THE STRESS LESS BUSINESS OWNER

THE STRESS LESS BUSINESS OWNER

10 Guiding Disciplines for a Stress Less Business and Life

Todd Hopkins

THE STRESS LESS BUSINESS OWNER
10 Guiding Disciplines for a Stress Less
Business and Life

Printed in the United States of America

Published by

At The Cross Publishing

ISBN: 978-0-9746671-5-7

Paperback, 2017

Scripture quotations marked (NIV) taken from the Holy Bible:
New International Version

This book is available for bulk purchases,
For information call 727-754-5990
Or email the author at:
ToddHopkins@OfficePride.com

Cover Design by Jeff Burridge and Leslie Ogle

First Edition

10 9 8 7 6 5 4 3 2

DEDICATION

To all the Business Owners out there who need to Stress Less! Also to our Office Pride franchisees, as you collectively seek to become the happiest people on the face of the earth.

TABLE OF CONTENTS

INTRODUCTION

Stress is a killer. People are dying everyday due to stress related illnesses. We were not created and our bodies were not designed to carry the stress burdens common to today's typical man or woman.

I know. As a 46 year old business owner, in the summer of 2012, my doctor looked me in the eye and said you are either in the middle of a heart attack or about to have one. My blood pressure and EKG were going crazy and he ordered me to the emergency room. There, as a team of doctors quickly surrounded me, attaching tubes, asking questions and running test, I asked myself how did I get here. I am a blessed man. I have a wonderful wife, great kids and a good business. I love the Lord with all my heart. Surely, this isn't how it ends for me, dying of a stress laden heart attack in a hospital emergency room.

Logically, I knew I shouldn't be stressed, but my body and heart were not being logical. I found myself constantly reliving negative situations in my life, especially as a business owner. I could have 99% happy employees, customers and franchisees and I would think about the 1%. t's not a good place. My body responded by dropping weight to an unhealthy level as I lost my appetite. I knew I was in trouble.

Through prayer and God's grace, I lived and am now living a stress less life. While a stress free life is not realistic, there are definitely things we can do or disciplines we can embrace to stress less. I have found that the stress less life is more enjoyable than the stressful life. Plus, I feel better, have more fun, appreciate life more and make better decisions. And the cherry on top is that I sleep well. I used to hate waking up in the middle of the night worrying about burdens. Those days have passed. In fact, it was during one of those sleepless nights that I finally asked myself, "Does it have to be this way?" and "What needs to happen for it to not be this way?" My answer was to seek and discover how to eliminate (or drastically reduce) stress in my life. How can I be more intentional about living a stress less life?

In this book, I will share with you the ten disciplines I discovered to reducing stress and bringing joy back to my life and business. I hope and pray the disciplines in this book will help you achieve the stress less quality of life you seek, and even to a level you never knew was possible.

Stress Less,

Todd Hopkins

PROLOGUE

The tie was a mistake; he shouldn't have listened to Claire. It was easier for her. In her knee-length black linen dress and sandals she looked appropriate but still could breathe. Linen was a good summer fabric. Bill needed to breathe. The collar was suffocating.

Only a funeral would get him to wear socks and a dark grey suit on a humid, airless summer morning. It was a recipe for heatstroke.

Bill's heart started to pound in his ears. Looking down through the assembled crowd at the hole in the ground, he couldn't reconcile the casket about to be lowered with his best friend Pete inside. It didn't seem real. Just last Saturday they were playing golf together. Pete seemed perfectly normal. A bit overweight around the middle, but you'd never guess he'd have a heart attack a few days later. Maybe it was time to cut down a bit. Claire kept bugging him to lose weight and he kept eating more just to annoy her.

Bill felt a beefy slap on his back. He turned towards a face that looked familiar but he couldn't quite place. Ah, yes, it was Matt's football coach. He nodded in silence as the coach kept walking to the other side of the gathering. What was his name? He couldn't remember. Is this what happens when you are about to turn fifty?

Anyway, it was nice of him to come. He didn't remember if the coach knew Pete well. They crossed paths often, they went to the same church, but he didn't know much about him.

Bill's knees started to feel as if they were filled with hot water instead of bone. If he collapsed right here it would do the others no favors. He would have to turn away and find a spot of shade hoping no one would notice. He crept backwards a few steps away from the mourners, stepping softly and flat on the ground. Just then someone sobbed loudly. Bill was glad for the diversion. He walked a few yards to the path, avoiding the gravel to not make a crunching noise, and collapsed on the nearest bench under a willow tree. He tore off the tie as if breaking free of a rattlesnake, took off his jacket and unbuttoned his collar.

"This South Florida heat can suck the life right out of you," said a soft voice behind him. Before he could turn, the voice had joined him on the bench. It was Conrad, a fellow businessman and churchgoer. They had crossed paths on several fundraisers and always seemed to end up together as they were both entrepreneurs.

"I feel like a limp twig leaving just now," Bill said.

"No need to apologize, we all know how much Pete meant to you," Conrad's velvet tone didn't match his tall broad-shouldered frame; Bill had always found it funny that such a tall man could be as gentle as a bunny.

"Maybe it all got to me," Bill shook his head in disbelief.

"I saw you looking a bit out of it, so I followed you to check that you were okay," said Conrad "I hope you don't mind."

They sat in silence for a while. In the distance the cadence of the pastor saying a final graveside prayer reached them, but Bill couldn't make out the words. Imperceptibly, his shoulders tightened. The air refused to enter his lungs. His eyes stung, burning. He looked over with wet eyes at Conrad.

"At the end of the day," Conrad said, "Pete would have wanted you to look after your health before anything else."

And that's when it came. The use of the past tense. Conrad didn't say "wants" he said 'wanted". His friend Pete, the brother he never had, divorced, no children, now belonged in the past tense. They would never have a present or a future tense together. The wave came from inside, the deep, shaking, raw sort of crying that you never want to witness in close proximity. All of Bill's emotions rippled out into one heaving uncontrollable fit of wet sobbing.

"I'm so sorry," is all Bill kept repeating, "I'm so sorry... I'm so sorry."

Conrad looked at his feet and simply placed a hand on Bill's shoulder and gripped it firmly. After a while the rise and fall of Bill's shoulders started to slow down.

"I'm not sure I was there for him, Conrad," Bill said, "I was so busy with my own stupid worries and my business, always rushing here and there. I've been so stressed out. I'm not sure I paid enough attention to Pete. What if I could have helped him?"

Conrad kept his hand on Bill's shoulder, his eyes down.

"My number is up next, I just know it," Bill said. "The way my life is going, I'm afraid I'll be down in the ground lying next to Pete before my next birthday. I've made such a mess of everything."

Conrad removed his hand and turned a little towards Bill. He hummed a few times, nodded to himself as if deciding whether or not he should say what he was about to say next. Maybe the funeral was the wrong place and time. But he went ahead anyway in almost a rehearsed kind of way.

"Stress and fear are big problems in today's world, Bill. Many people are being defined by the stress and worry in their lives. It is not how we were meant to live. I've been there."

Bill looked at Conrad sideways. Where was this coming from? What did this successful, powerful, forty-ish, healthy man know about stress and worry? He was as close to perfection as anyone could hope to achieve. He was a pillar of society, a devoted family man, and an outstanding entrepreneur. Anyway, why is he bringing this up all of a sudden?

Conrad continued, "There is a better way... a way to eliminate most of the stress and worry in our lives, allowing us to experience life the way it was meant to be, full of peace and joy."

Bill shuffled his feet. His nose was about to drip. Could this whole scene get more embarrassing? Not only had he disgraced himself in front of a well-respected man he barely knew, but he would have some awful dribbling episode as well. He was struggling to concentrate on what Conrad was saying.

"The first priority should be looking after your health and putting in place some simple routines that can reduce your stress. You still own a business, right?" Conrad asked, remembering that Bill had been quite charitable and involved in the community in years past.

Bill nodded slowly, trying to keep his nose from dripping.

"Great. The key is in systems and disciplines. As businessmen we know how to put in place systems for our business so we don't have to keep going back and doing some of the same things over and over again. Yet we don't apply the same principle to our life. In business, systems can help us prevent the same mistakes from reoccurring - the same goes for life. By being disciplined with certain routines and good thinking, we can eliminate repeating mistakes that create a lot of stress in our life. In fact, making a mistake a second time typically causes more stress than it did the first time because you not only have the stress presented by the mistake, you also have the frustration of knowing that you have allowed it to happen again."

Wait a minute here. Was Conrad reading his mind? Bill forgot all about his dripping nose and disheveled appearance and was now paying full attention to what Conrad was saying.

"Good personal routines, thinking and planning should produce great disciplines that ultimately contribute to stress reduction for all aspects of your life", Conrad said, punctuating his words with gentle hand gestures. It was hypnotic. "An example of a great routine is to simply remind yourself of where your business fits into your overall life picture. A business should not be running your life, it should serve to help you get where you want to go, or to help you serve God better, or to help you provide the type of lifestyle you want for your family. For many business owners, however, the business has overtaken them. It's very stressful to try to keep up with where the business is taking you, which often is a place where you never wanted to go – a place full of stress."

Bill was able to find his voice again. "How is it possible that running a huge business like yours, many times bigger than mine, you are not stressed?"

Conrad pressed his hand on Bill's shoulder.

"I'm glad you asked that," Conrad said. "You have no idea how great it is to hear that question. Just a few years ago it would have seemed impossible, until I ..."

Conrad stopped as they noticed that the gathering was starting to break up, the first few couples were already heading for their cars.

"Oh, man, I have to get back to Claire," Bill rising to his feet, "She'll be wondering where I am. Maybe we can continue our conversation later?"

"Sure," Conrad still relaxed on the bench, "how about lunch tomorrow?"

Bill hesitated. He had just meant later as an open-ended statement, as in some other indefinite time, if ever.

"That's awfully kind of you, I'd love to, but it's just been... hectic with the business these past few weeks. I don't stop for lunch. I get a sandwich brought in... if I'm lucky."

"No problem," Conrad rising from the bench to stand next to Bill, "I can deliver your sandwich."

What was it with this guy? Couldn't he take a hint? Bill felt guilty at the discomfort of being annoyed by kindness. The timing was just bad. Now that his eyes were clear of tears he noticed what Conrad was wearing. It was something between a shirt and a jacket. It looked crisp and high quality. They started walking back to where the others were dispersing.

"Is that linen?" Bill asked, attempting to steer the conversation from the subject of lunch. "It is," Conrad smiled, as if sharing a momentous secret, "It's a modern take on the traditional Guayabera. Perfect for this weather. I know the lady who owns the business that makes these, smashing success, quite a businesswoman. Hey, are you sure you don't want to change your mind about the sandwich? If you come to lunch with us you could meet her! I think you'd enjoy that. The food's not bad either."

Here we go again with the lunch business. Why had he said 'us'? Since when was this a group invitation? How many people was 'us'? More importantly, who was 'us'? Maybe he should go, because then he could be in and out quickly. If Conrad came to his business who knows how long he'd stay. He didn't seem to be in a rush for anything, which was odd, seeing that he owned one of the largest businesses in the county.

"I guess, maybe..." Bill said.

"Fantastic!" Conrad said as he swiftly started walking away "Do you know Green's Diner on the boardwalk? See you there at noon."

"Can't wait."

"Oh, Bill," Conrad called out and gestured "upstairs... upstairs..."

Bill nodded. He wasn't sure how to take Conrad's invitation. He was always friendly in church meetings, but more in a functional way of getting things done than in a socializing-let's-be-buddies way. Bill rejoined Pete's graveside with his jacket and tie in one hand. The last few people were leaving and he was glad for a moment alone. He squatted down, placing his free hand on the cool marble stone, which surprisingly was already on site. In the distance he saw Claire with his 12-year-old son Matt, talking to the minister and his wife. Claire looked as if she hadn't even noticed Bill's absence, and Matt looked as always, in a constant state of repressed irritation, as if he'd rather be anywhere else other than wherever his parents were.

Seriously Pete... why did you have to leave so soon? If anyone deserved to live it was you. Then he noticed the inscription in the stone: "Proverbs 3:5-6." Bill made a mental note to look up that scripture.

CHAPTER 1

Discipline to Replace Bad Emotions
With Good Emotions

"Where's Matt?" Bill called out from the front door.

"Tennis camp!" Claire said from the kitchen.

"How did he get there?" "Bike!"

"I don't think so. Bike's still in the garage."

"But he came down and had breakfast," Claire said, halfway through loading the dishwasher.

Bill went back inside and climbed the stairs. He better not be asleep, not again. Yep, there he was. Matt's chestnut curls were just peeking from under the cover. He had gone down to the kitchen, ate breakfast, and pretended to leave, then sneaked back up to bed. This meant that Bill was going to be late getting to the office. Again.

Bill hesitated at the door. He went down to the kitchen to ask Claire to drive Matt to tennis camp. He couldn't possibly be late again for the weekly staff meeting. Claire didn't reply, just quietly disappeared upstairs. Bill had already driven Matt to camp twice. Thank goodness school was starting again in a week. He knew he should be wishing to spend more time with his son, but right now the reality is that it was just time he didn't have. Plus Matt seemed to resent his presence so maybe it worked out best if he was fully occupied. What on earth was so difficult about getting breakfast, grabbing a racket and pedaling a few miles down the road?

On his way to work, Bill kept thinking back to what Conrad had said about how we were not meant to live with stress and worry. He wasn't looking forward to the lunch appointment with Conrad. He mentally ran through a list of possible excuses to cancel.

Meetings running late, illness, car trouble. All made him feel like a weasel.

"Mornin' boss!" Eamon greeted Bill from the office kitchen area, in his unmistakable Irish accent.

Eamon was Bill's right hand. He had moved to Florida ten years ago to marry his student exchange sweetheart after a 5-year long-distance relationship. He had started as a part- timer at Bill's company, White Tiger Cleaning Services, taking care of bookkeeping and admin duties, and gradually became indispensable to running the business. He had a rare combination of business savvy and people skills. Above all, he was deeply, thoroughly decent.

"What's on the menu?" Bill asked, forever teasing Eamon on his health-conscious habits.

"Let's see here, today we have two kiwis and a banana, and a homemade oatmeal muffin. A nice cup of organic fair-trade coffee. Sounds good."

It did sound good. Not the food itself, but the fact that his wife packed him a healthy breakfast every morning so that he would start the day off right. She always slipped him a little note or a funny cartoon, or a fortune cookie.

"There's another wee little glitch with the new accounting software," Eamon said. Somehow in his intonation it didn't sound so little.

"How little?" Bill said. He could feel his shoulders tightening even though he hadn't heard the news yet.

"Epic."

Here we go again. Just another day at the office. Now Bill had a genuine excuse to get out of Conrad's lunch. He cancelled his staff meeting and spent the entire morning trying to understand why the new software had completely scrambled their accounts receivable, why the backup didn't work, and why the software developer was nowhere to be found. Yet, in spite of the wrecked morning, Bill was not exactly sure why he hadn't just cancelled lunch. And so Bill found himself, at noon exactly, at Green's Diner.

"I'm expected," Bill said to the server, "... upstairs?"

"Bill?" the voice came from behind the counter, as if from a hidden speaker. Then the owner of the diner, Syd Green, unfurled his six-foot-two frame up from where he had been crouching to write the daily specials on the board. "Follow me".

They went back out the front door and around the back on the dockside, entering a private dining room adjacent to the main one but with its own private entrance and a tranquil view of the marina.

"I think it's supposed to be upstairs?"

"It's on the ground floor, 'Upstairs' is just the name the group reserves under, so we know to save the special table."

15

As the wide French doors opened Conrad greeted Bill with arms thrown wide. There were about six other people on a low U-shaped seating area made of sun-bleached wood around tables of the same material. Bill recognized a few faces, including the coach whom he still couldn't name. Everyone greeted Bill and nodded, signaling him to an empty spot in the center of the U.

"That's OK, I'll just sit here, I can't really stay long" Bill said, walking to a seat on the side.

"But you're our guest of honor!" said Conrad, "We are all so thrilled you could make it." Bill didn't want to be rude, so he sat in the assigned spot. They all quickly introduced each other just by first name, half of whom Bill would not remember, but that was fine since he'd probably never see them again. They passed around the food. The table was laid out with platters and salads, and pitchers of homemade lemonade. When he was a little boy, Bill's favorite thing in the world was to get his Mom to pack a picnic for him and Pete and a couple of neighborhood friends, and take it up to his tree house where a simple peanut-butter and jelly sandwich with lemonade felt like the most exotic feast. Suddenly he remembered this feeling deep inside, that sense of a carefree open road, of time slowing down and stretching the afternoon eternal.

"We start without waiting for anyone," Conrad said, "whoever gets here first just digs in."

The platters were passed around, everyone chatting and sharing, and Bill started to feel like he did in the tree house again. Which was odd to Bill, because these people were not his friends. There's a reason for the saying that food is the shortest road to a man's heart.

Food has a way of bringing people together. Bill thought of Eamon's packed breakfast, the picnics at the tree house, or grilling burgers in his backyard with his family when Matt and the girls were little. At home now it seemed like they were forever dining out, defrosting something, or ordering delivery.

"So, is this some kind of intervention?" Bill said.

"Maybe..." said Conrad, "we have nothing against sandwiches but, you know, we thought you needed to be rescued."

Bill had a forkful and suddenly his eyes widened. "Mmmwow..." he mumbled as soon as he finished the first bite. "This is amazing!"

There were knowing smiles and heads nodding around the table. The food was spectacular, in a simple, understated, best-you-ever-had way. At that point someone else arrived, waved hello and joined the table as if he had been there all the time. The conversation centered on the food, until the owner Syd came back and joined them. "The food is delicious," Bill said to Syd, "I had no idea. Since it's called a diner, I expected meatloaf and pies."

"Thank you," Syd said, "my Mom's side of the family is from Greece, and I grew up with this food. I'm glad you like it."

"I'm not sure what I'm eating," Bill said.

"That's the octopus salad, it has a name we can't pronounce", Conrad said.

Bill swallowed. He didn't remember ever eating octopus before. But there was a first time for everything and this was just unbelievably tasty. The stuffed peppers were beyond description. Bill felt his phone buzz twice in his chest pocket.

"Do you guys eat here often?"

"About once or twice a month, it depends."

"Depends on what?"

"If anyone of us is stressed and needing a reminder." Conrad said, as if that was a natural follow up to the question.

"Reminder?"

"What it takes to stress less. There are disciplines we follow. At the moment I think we have nine."

Bill put down his fork and knife and raised his hands in surrender.

"Okay people, let me have it. I was right. It is an intervention. Just come out with it. Who put you up to this?"

"I think in a way it is an intervention" Syd said, "but not for you. It's an ongoing intervention for all of us, by all of us. You see, we are all business owners. I have this diner and the catering business, as you know Conrad his real estate development thing, Diane has her apparel company, then Coach Kenner here. You know him from school but he also runs two sports store franchises. So we share some things we've learned along the way, we remind each other of our disciplines and we pretty much keep each other from straying too far off the path."

As Syd was explaining, everybody kept eating, relaxed, as if they've heard this a hundred times. It was odd for Bill, and yet it made sense at the same time.

"And you suddenly thought that these 'disciplines' might help me," Bill said.

"In a sense," Conrad said, "though it wasn't quite just my idea. But these disciplines, you know, they seem to work for every one of us, and we've shared them in the past. But it's all up to each one of us, really, if you're open to possibly thinking in a new way and changing some habits, you know."

Bill's phone was buzzing again. He moved it from his chest pocket to the back pocket of his pants.

"Such as?"

"Eating well," Coach Kenner laughed.

"I'm making a head start," Bill said, tucking in. He was aware that he was eating too enthusiastically for a polite first meeting, but the food was irresistible.

"But seriously," Conrad said, "it is possible to run a business without stress. Or, rather, it is possible to stress less by practicing disciplines to help us focus on what is really significant. We are entrepreneurs but we are human beings first. We need to look after our health, and our emotional and spiritual well-being, as well as our bottom line. Stress can kill all of these.

I once heard my pastor say that we are not human beings having a spiritual experience, but spiritual beings having a human experience. When a spiritual being begins to see itself as a human being, stress inevitably follows. We can't neglect our physical and emotional health, but our understanding of and response to the circumstances in our life on earth should manifest from a spiritual view, not physical or mental. Our desire should be to see God's perspective and how he is working, not immediately judge or stress over everything that comes our way."

"We see that in the news every day," Syd wiped the corner of his mouth, "people obsessing about their physical appearance, or material achievements, and yet they are still deeply dissatisfied with their lives."

"I hear what you're saying," Bill said, "but isn't it natural for me to want to provide for my family in every way I can? When something keeps me from doing my best, then I stress. It's life. It's normal."

What keeps me from doing my best?

"Yes," Conrad answered, "but how we view our need to provide can be problematic and stressful."

"That sounds nice," Bill softly defended. "I know you all mean well, but the thing is that sometimes life just takes over. Business is slower, customers start to leave,

21

employees expect to have a job, and your family is used to a certain way of life, and then well you stress."

"How do you normally deal with stress, Bill? What do you do?"

"I used to call Pete, my best friend, and he'd always have a funny story, and we'd go golfing, and I was still stressed but with less of a sharp edge."

"We all share in your grief Bill," Syd said, "You must miss your friend. We were all very fond of Pete, he had such a good heart."

"Not quite good enough as it turned out," Bill said, and immediately regretted his sarcasm. "I'm sorry, that was uncalled for, I don't know why I said that, I am not myself lately."

"No need to apologize," said Conrad, "I was thinking of what you said earlier about Pete. It seemed he knew how to help you apply one of our disciplines, which is the discipline to replace bad emotions with good emotions. This often requires you to separate the external situation from your internal response. Like what you just did, you knee-jerked to an external situation with sarcasm. But you could also choose to be gracious, or forgiving, or indifferent, or any number of responses. I think Pete knew this."

"Did he?" Bill said, "Pete was an uncomplicated kind of fella."

"It's not complicated at all," said Conrad, as if reading his mind. "It's very natural. We do it all the time in our personal lives, but we forget to apply it at work. As business owners, it

Discipline to Replace Bad Emotions with Good Emotions

is critical to learn how to manage stress. As I look at business owners I know and compare those who are successful to those who are not, there does seem to be a noticeable difference in how they manage stress. People who struggle with business tend to let stress manage them. A good question to ask yourself the next time you're experiencing stress is: How can I turn this around? How can I manage stress instead of it managing me? We believe the answer is in separating the external situation from the internal response."

"Which isn't that easy," Bill said.

"Not at first, granted. But it becomes second nature after a while. If properly managed internally, what would have been an externally stressful situation can actually become a learning experience. I went through this process once when a business disagreement ended up in mediation. That would have been stressful for me years ago. I chose to prepare, do my best, and be open to learn from the experience. I knew that the more I learned from the experience and process, the better I would be at my job as CEO. On the flight home, I took notes as to what I did well, could have done better and how I could be better prepared next time. It was a great learning opportunity and confidence builder. I chose to replace being stressed with an attitude to learn."

"So what Conrad is saying is that you have a choice," Syd confirmed.

"Sounds to me that what you're saying is that we can regain control over what happens," Bill said.

"Hah! Control!" said Coach Kenner, "I can't even get a bunch of strappy teenagers to control a tiny little ball, no matter how hard they train. But it doesn't mean we can't still play a good game. To some degree, control is an illusion. Those who believe they have control of their life are probably more foolish than wise. They are living in a dream."

"Exactly," said Conrad, "So, why stress over it? It's not about gaining control over what happens in our life, it's about choosing to control our response. If your plane is delayed, you can fret and complain and make a scene, or choose to use the time productively and read, sleep, work on your laptop or have a good conversation with a fellow stranded passenger. Both ways you'll arrive at the same time at your destination. If properly managed internally, what would have been an externally stressful situation can actually become a positive experience."

"About five years ago," said Coach Kenner, "you may remember, we had the high school basketball team doing surprisingly well, which let's face it, we always were quite terrible. We had almost upset the state champions. When we found ourselves with a nice lead in the fourth quarter, we got nervous about the possibility of winning and feared blowing the lead that we were not supposed to have. Stress kicked in and kids just started making bad decisions and bad passes. Five or six turnovers later, we lost the game. We started worrying about the outcome and failed to finish playing the game. What I took from that is that if we could have only been mature enough to embrace the challenge, play our best and trust God with the outcome, we would have been less stressed and the result may have been different. I know they were just kids, but that's when we learn these bad habits, and the same principle applies now. So we were talking about the game later, having one of our Upstairs meetings, and we said what would happen in our life if, rather than trying to take control and worrying or stressing about the outcome, we could embrace the challenge, do our best and trust God with the results? Let's make that heart and mental adjustment now rather than wait ten years to look back and wish we had done it sooner. So we did."

"Interestingly, stress is often our response to a perceived or actual threat," Conrad said. "Note that I didn't say actual, but perceived or actual. This means that many times we worry and stress over perceptions that are not even real. We worry for nothing. I once read that 90% of the things people worry about never happen."

"Try it next time you're stressed," said Coach Kenner, "like I tell the kids when someone provokes them they don't have to hit back. I tell them they can choose patience, but it is easier for them to understand if I tell them to take out the bad emotion and replace it with another emotion, a good or positive emotion that will not get them in trouble. Like replacing a flat tire. You don't just keep driving on three wheels, you put a tire in its place, even if it's a spare, and it's not forever, but it'll get you to where you were going and keep you out of the ditch."

"That helped us all a great deal," Conrad finished chewing, "the idea of replacing one emotion with another. I mentioned earlier that on a delayed flight you could choose patience. I believe it is easier to choose to not stress if we can pick something else in its place. For example focusing on patience and love instead of stress is easier than just trying not to stress. It's like our internal emotions are asking, 'If we can't stress, what should we do instead?' If you provide the answer, you can move on from the negative to the positive. Tell your emotions to be patient and show love. Anything positive is better than stress. The fruit of the Spirit listed in Galatians 5:22-23 is a good place to start. You can choose from any of the fruit of the Spirit: love, joy, peace, patience, kindness, goodness, faithfulness, gentleness and self-control."

Bill fell silent. He stared at the center of the table, and then slowly, methodically, arranged his napkin, his glass. With his pinky finger he swept up a few stray breadcrumbs into a neat little pile, then picked them up one by one and put them onto his plate. He finally set down his fork and knife. When he looked up around him, the back of his eyes had started to sting.

"I feel like I need to set something straight," said Bill, "especially to you, Syd." Syd leaned slightly forward, his eyes meeting Bill's.

"When you expressed your sympathy for Pete's death, just then," Bill continued, "what I really meant to say is that I appreciate it. Thank you. You've all been very kind, you've shown me kindness, and I am now choosing to take your first discipline to heart and replace my sarcasm with gentleness. That's what you've done for me today. It's hard for me to see how any of this could help you guys run your businesses, but I've certainly enjoyed the food and the company."

With that, Bill said his goodbyes and left, stopping on his way out at the counter to pay his share. His first thought out the door was how he would tell Pete about his strange experience, and what he might say. When he realized that this was not possible his eyes were stinging even more. The last thing he wanted was to start crying in public places. The conversation had made him so emotional. What a peculiar bunch. And what's with the "Upstairs" codename? He forgot to ask. Anyhow. They meant well, but how far all that talk was from the reality of his business and personal turmoil, they would never understand. He looked at his phone; there were about a dozen notifications just in the one hour that he had been away. Time to get back to reality.

At the table, Conrad and the rest were also getting up to leave for their respective businesses.

"I think we may have scared our friend Bill away forever," Coach Kenner said, slapping the table to raise himself up, "he must think we're all a bunch of loonies – just with pretty good taste in food."

"That may be the last we see of him," Syd laughed, nodding towards the door "he couldn't get away fast enough. You'll have to tell your "secret contact" who asked you to invite him that it didn't work."

Conrad smiled, and softly said, as if to himself, "Maybe; or maybe not. It's too early to say. I have a feeling he'll be back."

CHAPTER 2

Discipline to Work Ahead and Not Procrastinate

"I need a Guayabera" Bill said, downing his coffee in three long gulps.

"A what?" Claire assumed she misunderstood.

Bill wondered why he got up thinking about that this morning.

"It's a cross between a jacket and a shirt. Conrad was wearing one at Pete's funeral. In case you didn't notice, I almost fainted in the heat that day. Is Matt not up yet? He's going to miss the school bus."

"Be my guest," Claire said. Weekday morning routine had turned into slow-motion torture trying to get Matt up and ready for school. Gone were the days of sleepy but happy breakfasts and packed lunches. She glanced at the kitchen clock as if counting down the seconds until both father and son had left and she could reclaim the house to herself.

Bill climbed the stairs two steps at a time "Matt! You're going to be late!"

Not a sound. He wrapped his knuckles on the door.

"Come on buddy. Get a move on." Nothing.

Bill felt a rush of hot blood racing up around the back of his ears. He remembered the stress less discipline from the lunch group... replace a bad emotion with a good one. Ha! If only it were that easy. One of the fruit of the spirit is self-control. What if the disciplines don't work?

Okay. There has to be a way to raise a teenage boy without developing a heart condition. He pushed away his irritation and replaced it with benevolence. This is my son. I love him. I love him. I love him.

He went back to the kitchen and grabbed his mobile phone from his briefcase. He texted his own son upstairs. "If not dressed + breakfast in 3 minutes = 2 days no internet and no phone. Love, Dad" As soon as the text swooshed 'sent', there was a rustling from Matt's bedroom door opening.

"Morning honey," Claire kissed the top of Matt's ruffled hair and placed a bowl of cereal in front of him. Claire's eyes could change so quickly. From a pool of deep ocean blue Bill could swim in, they could harden into a cold steel mirror where he'd rather avoid his own reflection. But they were always a beautiful ocean pool when she looked at Matt.

Their son mumbled his thanks and ate his cereal with one hand while texting on his phone with the other. What could be so urgent this early in the morning?

Bill caught a glimpse of the school bus driving by. Not again. He'd have to drive Matt in the exact opposite direction from his work. He would be late to the office again, as he had been already five times in the last two weeks of school before the summer break. He'd have to nip this new bad habit in the bud.

"Claire, do you think you could drive ..." Bill could have sworn that Claire had just clenched her pupils, though he wasn't sure that was an actual physical possibility.

"Plumber's coming..." she said, turning her back to continue chopping fruit "Mattie, I'll pick you up from school for your dentist's appointment".

"That sounds nice," Bill said, thinking out loud, "to sit in a dentist chair would give me at least thirty minutes of not having to deal with phone calls, emails or tardy teenagers."

"You'd rather be at the dentist than doing your job?" Matt said, without looking up from his phone.

"What I mean is that, it's an excuse to switch off and let go. There's nothing else you can do in a dentist chair, you know, it's out of your control" Bill said.

"That's messed up." Matt said, just stating a fact, without any of his usual sarcasm.

"You bet, buddy, it is messed up. You have no idea to what degree."

As Bill leaned in to kiss Claire goodbye she presented her cheek but didn't kiss him back. The tip of his briefcase barely touched the chopping board where Claire was preparing a large fruit salad for a luncheon with her Bible study group. The wooden slab skidded like a hockey puck across the wet counter nudging Claire's favorite crystal bowl, which slid off the counter as if in slow motion and met the floor with a spectacular crash sending shards of glass, blood-colored juice and bits of sticky fruit all over the kitchen floor and onto Bill's shoes. It looked like a crime scene.

"Well for someone who runs a cleaning business you sure know how to make a mess," Claire said, pretending to smile through it.

"I'll clean it up," Bill said. He felt the blood rushing back around his ears again for the second time this morning. So much for benevolence.

Claire waved him off the kitchen floor. "I'll get it. You're already late!"

As Bill went through the foyer he made a mental note to buy Claire a pretty crystal bowl, then he noticed all the family photos from the picture wall had been taken down and stacked inside a cardboard box. From the open top Bill could see his own face grinning back at him from a heavy silver frame. He looked content, blessed, hugging Claire and Matt tightly against him while their two older daughters folded their arms around their shoulders. He remembered that moment three years ago skiing in Colorado. Matt was laughing, his head thrown back. Claire looked the picture of health, beautiful and beaming, resting her head on Bill's shoulder. Bill looked his best athletic self, slightly tanned, confident, quietly proud.... He looked... thankful. It was a wonderful family picture, a "group" picture as Bill had always been so notorious for promoting at family, friend and work gatherings. It was the last vacation they had taken as a family.

It now looked so far away, unreal, as if he were looking at an ad in a magazine.

"What happened to the picture wall?" Bill called out to Claire.

"Plumber needs to fix the leak in the guest washroom, he said it would be quicker to go through that wall." Claire called out, "it won't be a lot of damage, and he said you'll be able to wallpaper right over it in a couple of hours."

Oh boy. Another DIY job to add to the list. Thank you very much. In fact, Bill had planned to repair the plumbing himself, but had put it off for weeks, creating tension and stress with Claire. Bill finally conceded to

Claire calling a plumber.

Bill drove Matt to school in silence, deep into his mental compilation of the day's to-do list. Not that it would do him any good these days as he always got to the end of the day without crossing off a single thing on the list. The tyranny of the urgent. Today, for example, the essential things he had to do for the business would have to wait because one of his top customers had asked him to come in for a meeting. Usually it was Bill who made the rounds visiting with his clients, stopping for a cup of coffee. Some of his clients he frequented socially, they had become friends. Today he also had the meeting with the software guys that muddled up the invoicing system, still not working after three weeks of runarounds.

When he got to the office there was the scene that greeted him almost every day now. People pacing outside his door, waiting to talk to him, a stack of phone messages.

Nothing in the way of chitchat from Eamon today. He was just sitting quietly across in his cubicle, no sign of breakfast. A courteous but clipped good-morning-boss and his head went back down to computer screen. He thought of the photos in the foyer at home. It felt the same here at work, as if all the joy and pride had been boxed up.

A text from Conrad came in. It just said "Upstairs. Noon." He hadn't seen or heard from Conrad or any of them since that lunch. He normally would have sent a little message of thanks following the lunch, but he didn't want to encourage a second invitation, and yet here it was. He thought it best to ignore it. That way he didn't have to lie. He was busy. Everybody knew he was busy.

When he got to his desk, there was a food container and a note. In the case was a muesli square and fruit salad. The little message said "Tarzan would only fight one alligator at a time." He laughed out loud. Eamon!

He had relinquished his breakfast, perhaps knowing that Bill had a tough day ahead.

"Thanks, man!" Bill called out.

"Don't thank me," Eamon said, "someone brought in muffins today. You inherited my breakfast."

"I like the note. Your wife is a wise woman," Bill said.

"That's why she married me, Boss!"

Bill set aside the fruit salad to open his emails, then caught himself, as if a voice inside his head had said: enjoy this food. It is a blessing. He opened the container and savored the fruit slowly. Peach, apple, blueberry. Bill thought back to the delicious food at Syd's diner. What did he have to lose if he went out for lunch? One hour? Would they have that octopus salad again?

"Right. Let's see which alligator comes first." he said out loud, for Eamon's benefit.

So which alligator would come first? Bill pulled out a yellow pad and a thick marker and wrote a big #1 "Replace bad emotions with good emotions". He pinned it to his message board, then started a 'to-do' list. Alligator 1: software guys, Alligator 2: customer meeting, before he got to number 3, Eamon walked in.

"Software guys can't make it today," Eamon said.

"Are you serious? Why?"

"Didn't say, they just emailed."

"This is getting ridiculous," Bill said, "I keep waking up in the middle of the night in a cold sweat, and these guys don't seem to care at all. They dropped us in the middle of it, and now they go missing."

"Pretty much," Eamon said, "I don't know what to think."

"I'm thinking the only way is to sue," Bill said.

"What, to get a reaction?" Eamon said.

"But then the risk is that they may string it along and we'll end up paying a fortune in legal fees and still not get the system working."

"Needs a bit more good thinking," said Eamon.

"Maybe it's more like correct thinking," Bill said. "My new friend Conrad would add that it is correct thinking from God's perspective, as it relates to our spiritual beings."

Eamon was slightly surprised that Bill was mentioning God. He was usually the first one to bring up God in conversation, not Bill.

"So, in other words, how would God want you to handle this?" Eamon asked.

"Yes, exactly. What opportunities, resources and discernment has God provided in this situation or decision that I am currently not seeing? It's the opposite of making a bad decision."

"You could pray," Eamon said, "you know, for good thinking, and sound judgment. Forgive me if it's none of my business, but you said that you're not sleeping well?"

"I can't remember the last time I slept through the night."

"That's a shame, boss. You know, when we are tired, we tend to make not so great decisions," Eamon said, "everything seems worse than it is. It's like the brain is not 'on'. So I wouldn't make any decisions until you get a good night's sleep."

"I know," Bill said, "it's just one thing after another. I sleep until around two or three am, and then I wake up running through a list in my head of everything that's going wrong.

By then I only have a little over an hour until Claire's alarm goes off, so I move to the den so I don't wake her up, then she doesn't like it when she finds me there in the morning, everybody starts the day cranky."

"That's your alligator number one: sleep. Switch off tonight, don't set the alarm, just sleep until you wake up naturally. The world and the business will still be here when you get up. I'll be here. Just get up slow, and I'll even let you borrow my little morning prayer: God, help me to have good thinking today and see people and situations through your eyes. After a good night's sleep those alligators on the list don't seem quite as big. You may be worrying about things that are not going to happen anyway."

"I'll try. I can't guarantee but I'll try. What time's the meeting with the three brothers?"

"Two."

"Still didn't say what it was about?"

"No, they said they preferred to discuss it with you in person."

"You haven't got any gut feeling?"

"Not a clue. Everything seems okay from our end. Maybe they want to bring us down in price?"

"Nah. Those guys are not the kind to nickel and dime you. We've already reduced services and lowered prices during the economic downturn, they should be pretty happy about that."

The three brothers were respected orthodontists that had garnered a nationwide reputation. White Tiger cleaned the office complex they owned, which housed their practice, plus a blood lab and two successful cosmetic orthodontists. The place was about five minutes from the boardwalk, and there was the nice gift-shop there, also, where he could pick up Claire's crystal bowl, grab a quick lunch and get to the meeting. He would knock out several alligators in one fell swoop.

"Bill!" The elegant lady in the gift shop was waiting for her gift to be wrapped.

"I'm sorry, I forgot your name." Bill recognized her from the lunch.

"It's Diane," she said, shaking his hand.

That would be easy to remember, she reminded him of Diane Sawyer.

"I smashed my wife's favorite fruit bowl today, I thought I might replace it." "They have such nice things here. Talking about nice things, Conrad said you complimented him on one of my Guayaberas."

"You make those? What a coincidence. I was just talking about it with my wife this morning," Bill said, "I was saying I should get one."

"You should come over to the showroom," Diane said, "we don't sell retail but for you we'll make an exception."

"I'd love to," Bill said, "as soon as I have a minute. Work's been crazy."

"Here's my card," Diane said, "just come whenever you're in the area. Anytime. Are you joining us for lunch today?"

Bill remembered Conrad's text. He had completely brushed it aside.

"Oh, I don't know, I'm having a bit of a day."

"It's almost noon already," Diane said, and moved to the door, "Plus the networking is good for you. I'm headed out there myself. Are you sure?"

He had time, the customer meeting wasn't until two. He was starving. It didn't make sense to grab a sandwich somewhere just to avoid this lunch, it felt petty. So that's how he found himself roped in again sitting at the U-shaped table, this time on the end nearest to the door. There was only Syd, Conrad, Diane and the coach. Same as last time, there was no waiting, they all started passing around the food and chatting immediately.

"So how's the disciplines thing going?" Bill asked, just to make conversation, "anyone need reminding?"

"Oh yes, I do actually," Diane said, "I always seem to struggle with the same discipline."

"What's that?" Bill felt relieved the focus would be on someone else today.

"We call it the discipline to work ahead," she said, "in other words, not to procrastinate. It used to be pretty bad with me, now it's much better, but every now and then I slip.

Take this morning for example. When I have something on my list that I really dread doing, I find myself going for a haircut - or like today, shopping for a gift - instead of doing what I needed to do, which is to sort out the models that we need to discontinue. I hate doing it, it's like picking which child you love least. I keep putting it off, and it creates a problem for my buyer to place orders for materials."

"That's a tough one," Bill said, "I'm guilty of the same. This morning I should have been exploring the legal recourses against a supplier that's giving us the runaround, and instead I was buying a fruit bowl."

Coach Kenner joined in, "At least procrastination is good business for the gift shop!"

They all laughed and shared stories of how in different degrees they had all put off something they dreaded doing at one time or another. "The thing is that procrastination is a luxury that most businesses can't afford," said Conrad. "So that's why we call this the discipline to work ahead and not procrastinate. The thought of this is terrifying to most of us. I couldn't think of a reason to work on anything for very long before it was due.

I have always been the type of person to wait to the last minute. You know the drill – study all night before an exam the next day. Then one day

> Discipline to Work Ahead and Not Procrastinate

before a presentation at a weekend event, I found myself holed up in my room and missed a wonderful opportunity for fellowship with potential clients during the afternoon free time. All because I was up in the hotel room preparing the presentation that I was going to deliver that evening. I had waited until the last minute. An associate of mine helping me with the graphics and powerpoint had no idea of what I was going to show or say, so I made her anxious. I promised myself it would not happen again. My colleagues and clients deserve better.

Procrastinating high priority items is not good. It creates stress and ultimately reduces quality. It has taken a lot of self-investment in reading and learning from my peers, but over the years I have developed the good habit of working ahead, and I owe it to these fine people around the table. At the same event the following year, you should have seen me.

I delivered the best presentation ever. I had practiced and polished it and what's best, my associate thanked me for giving her plenty of time to work on her part and prepare the handouts. Having more time meant that I had researched more interesting cases and examples, more pertinent material. Several people present commented on how useful and interesting it was."

"I provided my best quality because I worked ahead. I had more fun because urgency was eliminated which reduced my stress. Unless quality doesn't matter, and we like stress, we need to work ahead and not procrastinate."

"Can you think of any instance in your life where quality doesn't matter?" Conrad asked to nobody in particular.

"My software guys seem to think so," Bill said, thinking out loud, "they are not particularly bothered that their system has left White Tiger unable to access invoicing or even get access back to the old system. The patches don't work, they put off our meetings, as if they think ignoring the problem will cause it to go away by magic."

"Nightmare," Coach Kenner said, "who's the provider?"

"They are new young guys, I was giving them a chance and we are one of their first clients."

"That's a shame," Conrad said, "Let us know if there's anything we can do to help?"

"I will. Thanks again for your kindness. Great food once again Syd!"

--

Bill was feeling calmer after lunch, both from the effect of a full stomach and the good conversation. Nothing would have prepared him, however, for the intensity of the meeting with the three brothers. In about five minutes and without any small talk, they tag-teamed

Bill with a list of serious shortcomings. Items on the invoices that hadn't been carried out, such as several instances of floor buffing billed but not done, and even of greater concern, missing drugs from the locked cabinets in the lab. They had not notified White Tiger right away. Instead everything had been documented with details, dates and times. They were threatening to terminate their contract, were requesting refunds for work not performed and warned Bill that they may be forced to declare the missing medication if the matter was not resolved quickly.

As Bill left to go back to his office, his head was spinning in disbelief. Never in twenty years of business had his name or the name of White Tiger been linked to any sort of wrongdoing or ill intent. He could feel his heart beating in his chest, as his fingers wrapped around the wheel. He almost ran a red light as he tried to remember who were the cleaners assigned to the three brother's medical facilities. It couldn't be one of his team. There had to be a mistake somewhere.

"Eamon," he said to his second in command, and pointed with his chin towards his office.

"Not too good?"

"Epic."

CHAPTER 3

Discipline to Identify and Eliminate Stress Triggers

The world and its complications would have to wait for Bill. As he was driving back home on Friday evening, his left arm went numb, his neck felt hot, then started sweating cold. He pulled over on the side of the road and called Claire. The next hours were blurry; he remembered the sign on the emergency entrance, the smell of hospital grade cleaner and white shoes squeaking on terrazzo floors.

"We can go home now," Claire said, her eyes a pool of blue filled with concern for him.

Bill didn't say anything on the drive back home, and was surprised to see Matt sitting at the kitchen table. On Fridays he would be either joining his friends to watch movies or be cooped up in his room worshiping his tablet. Waiting there was Bill's favorite roast chicken and potato salad from the deli down the street.

"Oh honey, thanks for thinking about getting some food!" said Claire.

Matt shrugged with the tiniest smile on one corner of his mouth. His eyes were large and a soft hazel color.

"Well, let's eat!" Bill said.

He knew Matt was waiting for reassurance, that everything was all right, and his Dad wasn't sick and his world could go on as usual.

"Dad's fine," said Claire. "It was just a little scare."

"I just had a rough day in the office," Bill said, "that's all. Nothing a good night's sleep can't fix."

"Maybe you could take a few days off," said Claire.

"Absolutely. Tell you what. As soon as I get these few wrinkles ironed out at work we'll go for a weekend away. Now, let's eat, I'm starving."

Bill leaned over and wrapped one arm loosely around Matt's shoulders. He felt Matt's muscles melt under his touch as if he had been holding his breath for a long time. Such a mystery, parenthood. Bill had felt more confident raising girls, with Matt he mostly relied on Claire. They had said they would stop at two children but then after a gap of several years, Matt came as a surprise. Claire was radiant, and loved every minute with the new baby, but somehow Bill felt as if Matt was a different kind of responsibility, as if it was up to Bill to mold him into a man. He felt he would be a hero to his daughters, no matter what. With a son Bill felt as if there was something he was supposed to supply, only he didn't know what that was. In fact, these days, he felt like never before that the answers to everyday questions escaped him. Here he was, after years of building a successful business with a wonderful wife by his side, and three healthy, loving children, yet for no particular reason, everything he had built with so much effort was just slipping away like sand in an hourglass. The tighter he tried to hold on to it, the faster the sand ran out.

Dinner was a bit quieter than usual. Bill actually missed the daily tussle to get Matt to come downstairs to eat.

"So what happened?" Matt finally said.

"What do you mean?" Bill said.

"To you, at work."

"Oh Matt, that's not conversation for the table, Dad needs to rest," Claire said.

"No, that's okay," Bill said, "it's complicated Matt. It's not one thing, but a stack of little things that pile up on top of each other."

"Like what?" Matt was not going to give up.

Claire looked across the table and shrugged. Bill smiled. She shrugged the exact same way as Matt, one shoulder slightly higher than the other. He felt such love for his family; he ached to have his two older daughters who were away at college right here, around the table with him. It was a physical pang in his stomach.

"Here's the thing," Bill said. "For a few weeks we've been chasing the guys that sold us new software for our billing. You know what billing means, right?"

Matt rolled his eyes.

"Of course you know," Bill said, "so the software is a dud, it wiped out the entire backup files, and we don't know who owes us money, who's already paid, etc. They keep patching up the thing, but it doesn't work, and they are not accepting responsibility."

"Can you get another one?"

"Well, we paid a good bit of money for this one, and we were trying to help these new guys, anyway, that's one thing, and then another thing is a client accusing us of stuff that caught me off guard, things that I didn't know were going on, right under my nose."

"Like what?"

"Our guys are supposed to follow a strict routine, with optional extras, cleaning some medical offices, and they didn't do the work but still billed the extras," Bill swallowed hard, he still hadn't had time to process the bitter pill of the meeting with the three brothers. An uneasy feeling was coming back over him.

"Should you be talking about this?" Claire said, "The doctor said to take it easy for a few days."

"That's what they always say when they don't know what's wrong with you," Matt said.

Claire smiled and got up to get some grapes from the fridge. She placed them in the middle of the table and the three of them reached over picking the juicy sweet fruit. Bill acted as if he was going to spit the seed in Matt's direction.

"Dad!" Matt giggled, and picked a grape pretending to prepare for retaliation.

"Don't you two dare!" Claire laughed.

For an instant, Bill remembered the familiar sounds of his family. A little chaos, a great deal of laughter, clinking of tableware, voices wafting in and out of conversation. It only lasted a few seconds. When did it all go from happy chatter to broody silences and clipped exchanges? Bill couldn't quite put his finger on the moment it had changed.

Maybe when the girls moved out? Bill's head was so fuzzy. He had the feeling he had forgotten something today, but this was a feeling he was having often now. He kept forgetting the most trivial things.

"So, how do you know they did it?" Matt asked, after a while.

"Who did what?"

"Your guys, how do know they did what the customer says they did?" Matt said.

"Well, these three doctors have no reason to lie. They are educated, wealthy, upstanding professionals."

Matt shrugged again.

"Maybe they are not lying," Matt said, "but it's pretty easy to pick on the cleaners. What if they're wrong and it's just a mix-up?"

At that moment Bill's phone buzzed. A text message came in. Bill recognized Conrad's number.

You OK? Heard you were taken to hospital.

"Who's that?" Claire asked.

"Nothing, I'll reply later."

A cloud swept across Claire's eyes, then it was gone. Matt helped Claire clear the table and Bill took the chance to sneak a quick reply to Conrad. He left the phone on the table and went outside to get Claire's gift from the car. It wasn't there. That's what had been nagging him. He probably had left the package at the diner.

Claire saw Bill's phone screen light up on the kitchen table. She just caught a glimpse of the messages before it went out again. It said:

I'm OK, false alarm. Can't talk right now, but need to see you. Can we meet upstairs?

The reply said:

Glad to hear it. Upstairs Monday usual time. You left something behind today by the way.

Claire couldn't process what she had just read. *You left something behind?* Where had her husband spent the day? He said he was stressed from work... could it be possible that there was another reason? She was just glad that Matt hadn't noticed the messages.

When Bill came back the mood in the kitchen had dropped below arctic levels. Matt had gone upstairs to his room. Claire was wiping the counter mechanically, with slow strokes. Bill wished he had the gift to give to her, which would have cheered her up.

"So..." Bill said, "Now that Matt's out of earshot, what did the doctors say exactly?"

"Anxiety attack," she said. Her tone was clipped, distant. "You're scheduled for a follow up visit on Monday morning. They said you need to rest."

--

Monday morning back in the office, Bill smiled. He then answered a few emails and phone calls from home before his doctor's appointment. He emailed Eamon to call in the cleaners that worked on the three brothers building for a meeting in the afternoon, and to pull up their files and itemized logs of each job and the corresponding invoices to match. The doctor's visit was fairly smooth. All his vital signs were normal; the doctor prescribed some sleeping pills in case of need. Bill had never been a fan of pills, but on the other hand he knew he couldn't afford to keep waking up in the middle of the night. His body couldn't take it anymore. Even this weekend, trying his best to set aside time to wind down before going to bed, he still had not slept past four in the morning.

Today Bill was actually looking forward to the 'upstairs' meeting, not just for the food. For a change they were having the regular diner menu. There was a bowl with coleslaw, a platter of cold cuts, and Syd had just brought over a steaming meat loaf and mashed yams. Bill was reminded of the way he used to feel when he got together with Pete. He could be himself; he didn't have to pretend to have all the answers. All the seats around the table were full. Syd, Conrad, Coach Kenner and Diane, and five other people Bill still couldn't name properly.

"Thanks for coming today," Bill said, "I didn't know who else to talk to, I needed to ask you guys for your help. This would be Pete's job normally."

"Sure. We are glad you called, and that you're okay," Coach Kenner said.

set my pulse racing. I was transferring this sense of impending doom on to my whole family. It started to show. The kids in particular started to act up, and my wife and I weren't equipped to deal with it. Like most families, mornings were chaotic trying to get the kids up and ready for school."

"Tell me about it!" said Bill, "I could write the book on that."

"Well, imagine on top of that the closing emails from the evening before, listing all the operational and employee problems and issues. I went from one driving range to expanding into eight franchises in a very short time. Now I have eighteen. Anyhow, I went off on a tangent. I tend to do that. Either I'm totally quiet or you can't stop me for hours.... So I know there will always be something to go wrong when you start a new business but, Bill, I had this feeling that I could never get away from it. That if I took a day off something would go horribly wrong and I would let everybody down. I was telling myself that all I had to do was work through all the problems, then I would have some quiet time to plan for the business and not just the problems, and eventually I could start having fun again. I was fooling myself. I was on a treadmill.... I would go back home from work and slap my laptop on the table as soon as dinner was over, and then I felt like

I had just gone to sleep when the alarm would go off and it was time to get the kids up. I would check my email even before I brushed my teeth. My wife Sally needed help, the kids would start screaming, and before you know it Sally and I were screaming at each other. I believed Sally should be able to handle the kids while I'm trying to keep the business alive. Sally started looking for a job, not just to make ends meet but basically to get away from me and this robotic loop I had created. She had a job before and totally hated it, and she loved raising our family and looking after the home. Anyway, we started to blame the economy, the business, the industry, the government, and even the weather. One day blended into the next, and it didn't take long for us to start blaming each other. There was never any meaningful quiet time. The minute the kids were on the school bus and I headed to the driving range, Sally would just collapse on the sofa with exhaustion. Sometimes by noon she hadn't even changed out of her pajamas."

Between mouthfuls, Bill was nodding his head, or pointing at himself with his fork.

"Does any of this sound familiar?" asked James.

"School mornings," Bill said, "brutal!"

"One morning, we couldn't find shoes for one of the kids to wear," said James, "How could we lose a pair of shoes? So the bus is just around the corner and my repair guy is calling. I needed that equipment fixed before we opened. I could not believe the sound of my own voice, yelling at my own little kids. When they finally left, I looked at my wife and saw her face had turned white and she had tears in her eyes. She had two simple questions. She asked; 'Does it have to be this way?' and my answer in my gut was: no. Something had to give. Then Sally asked her second question: What needs to change for it not to be this way? Those two questions were all I needed to hear."

"So what did you do?" Bill asked.

We got in the car. I wasn't sure why but we drove to Home Depot. "We bought a huge shoe bin," James said, "Inexpensive, wood toy box. From that day forward we would never again have to look for shoes at the last minute. That eliminated our most immediate problem. The kids took all of five minutes to get it, as soon as they come in; they take their shoes off and put them in the bin. You may think it sounds minor and silly but somehow identifying that the shoes were a trigger helped us identify other minor little triggers as well. We just had to stop for ten minutes and ask what needed to happen for it to not be this way. Of course, this was just a small solution to a small part of the overall picture, but if you can eliminate 'noise' in one process or system it sets off a chain of events. You are in a more balanced space. From that simple little thing, I took the same approach with small triggers at work and implemented small improvements to the workflow. The evening emails from work now are marked 'action', 'need to know', or 'FYI', so I can handle them in order of priority. That way I know that if I don't get to read all the 'FYI' I can read them later and the sky is not going to fall."

"That sounds so simple," Bill said.

"The most effective solutions are the simple ones," Conrad said. "We always asked those two questions when a system gets stuck. So Bill, tell me, your anxiety for example, does it have to be this way? What needs to change for it to not be this way?"

Clearly, the answer to the first question was no, but Bill didn't quite have the answer to the second. How could he eliminate the stress trigger and enjoy his morning time with Matt and Claire without sacrificing efficiency at work?

Syd was now thanking everyone for coming, standing at the door, and as Bill left, he turned around to remind him about Claire's gift that he had left behind the week before. Syd went back to the office to retrieve it and handed the beautifully wrapped package over to Bill.

"Thanks Syd," Bill held it tightly, "I appreciate your holding it for me."

"Anytime. And don't stress about stressing. Eliminating much of the business related stress in your life can sometimes be only a few organizational or operational steps away. The Pareto rule would show that 80% of your stress is coming from 20% of your activities. If you can identify and improve just 10% that almost cuts your stress in half. While owning a fast growth business can have its perks, one of the downsides is that many times you can find yourself holding on and ending up in a place you had not planned to be, often feeling stuck and stressed. You just have to find your shoe bin, you know, the one that fits you. I would pray for clarity."

"Thank you Syd," Bill said, "I get it. I'll pray for clarity."

Bill turned around as he was leaving.

"One more thing, Syd," he asked, "what's with the 'upstairs' code name?"

Syd pointed to the sky. "You know, God... upstairs.

Just a reminder that we have a bigger purpose and stressing is not part of it."

Bill laughed. "Of course!"

"There's always two levels," Syd said, "and that also applies to our business. Whatever you do 'downstairs' in our world of emails and phone calls and software that doesn't work, it all has to be in harmony with the work that goes on 'Upstairs' in the business. You know, your mission, what we're really here for. If they don't go together, if they pull you in different directions, that's when things go off the rails."

"Upstairs," Bill nodded while grasping the concept.

"Yep." Syd smiled as he noticed Bill starting to understand, "that's what all these disciplines that we practice are really about."

"You guys are nuts," Bill called out, waving to Syd and smiling.

"I certainly hope so!" Syd called back.

Bill caught himself humming a song as he was driving back to his office. Wait a minute, he thought, I'm on my way to a potentially confrontational meeting with errant employees, and I feel like singing? Did Syd put something in that lemonade of his?

CHAPTER 4

Discipline to Get a Good Night's Sleep

In an instant, Bill's state of mind went from singing in the car to feeling his heart pounding between his ears. *Identify your triggers.* Well, Bill could safely say that people lying to his face was certainly a stress trigger.

"You didn't think to let us know about this mate?" Eamon asked a confused-looking janitor.

Still in his work gear, the middle-aged wiry man was shifting in his chair every few seconds. There was no reply.

"Denying it isn't going to help, you know," Bill said, "it was just a matter of time before it would come up. Anyway, let's cut this short. We're going to have to suspend you for a few days until we can make a decision. I'm sorry but I can't have you accessing their facilities anymore so I'm going to have to ask you for the keys."

Bill left Eamon to complete the paperwork and called the three brothers to let them know that they were taking disciplinary action until they could get to the bottom of the matter. "The thing is, Boss," Eamon said walking over to Bill's office, "with both employees denying everything, we can't really act until we have access to the correct billing history."

"Which brings me to our other nightmare," Bill said, "no news from the software guys?"

"No news," Eamon shrugged. "I'm out of ideas."

"Do we have any paper trail of this customer's invoices?"

Partial. We have all new invoices since the new system switch, but we don't have the historical. We could ask the customer for their copy of the invoices," Eamon offered with a tone of voice knowing that it was not a good idea.

"That makes us look even worse. Let me think about this." Bill put his hand on his head and briefly closed his eyes.

"Shouldn't you be taking it easy by the way Boss? Weren't you going to take a break?

"I'm fine. I'll take a break as soon as we sort these things out. Say, Eamon, do you ever wake up in the middle of the night, worrying about things?" Bill asked.

"No, I sleep like a brick. You're still having trouble sleeping?"

"Can't get my head around taking pills."

"Have you tried walking?" Eamon asked.

"What, like sleepwalking to the fridge?"

"No, I mean like walking, outside, during the day."

"What's that got to do with sleeping?" Bill clipped back.

"Helps a lot of people. I myself, find exercise extremely boring. I have to say it's one of the rare things I don't naturally excel at," Eamon said with a grin as he got up and gathered his paperwork. "But I've listened to enough business owners to know the energy they get from having a good exercise routine. So I walk. Short walk, long walk, doesn't matter. Once a day, every day, rain or shine. I take the dog, take the kids, alone, with the wife. When we are together we play I spy, when I'm alone, I give thanks for my family, my health, my job. Out loud. Seriously. People think I talk to myself."

Eamon walked out, then popped his head through the threshold. "Mainly I give thanks for my boss," Eamon said.

"And you were doing so well," Bill laughed.

Bill's phone buzzed with a text message from Matt. It was unusual these days for him to text his Dad, usually he would talk to Claire.

Wanna go fishing?

Bill didn't quite get Matt's message, maybe there was a joke to follow? Bill went along with it.

Sure. Sounds fun!

Nothing. No reply. Maybe Matt had sent the text in error and it wasn't meant for him.

--

When Bill got home that evening, later than usual, he found something blocking the front door. Finally when it budged, Bill saw that it was the carton with the photos that had been moved too close to the doorframe. The hallway was a war zone. The picture wall had disappeared behind a drop cloth, the floor was covered in plastic sheets, and there was white dust everywhere.

"Claire!" he called out.

"Come around the back!" she shouted.
Bill closed the front door and went around back and came in through the garage to the kitchen.

"I see the plumber was here," Bill said.

"Yep, and he had a little miscalculation, so pretty much half the wall needs to be redone." "Did he find the problem?"

"Not yet."

"Great. And what's the junk on the floor in the garage? Tell Matt to put that back up." "What do you mean? That's for your fishing trip," Claire said, her eyes widening. "What fishing trip?" Bill said, blinking rapidly.

"Oh, no-no-no," Claire said, "No-no. Not again."

Just then Matt came bouncing down the stairs waving a sleeping bag. He gave Bill a quick hug, a mundane gesture but something he hadn't done lately.

"Found it!" Matt said. "It was in my closet. Go figure."

"Hey buddy," Bill was not sure what to say, "You've been busy." Claire shot Bill a look that would have made a glacier cold.

"Yeah, I wanted to check that all the gear is still okay in case we need to borrow something."

"Good idea," Bill said, still not understanding, "so you want to run it by me one more time?"

"We go directly from school on Friday, Coach Kenner is picking you up at the office. So take all the stuff with you."

Matt disappeared again to the garage.

"So, did I know about this?" Bill asked Claire, still trying to figure out what he had just agreed to.

"It's the reward for the boys that volunteered to paint the church hall, remember? One of the parents is having an operation, can't make it so Matt texted you and you said sure, it'll be fun," Claire said, "don't you dare cancel on him, I haven't seen him this excited since pre-school."

Just what Bill needed? This was the story of his life. Customers threatening to cancel, a delinquent provider he wanted to sue but shouldn't, his house turning into a demolition site and what was the solution? Take a bunch of rowdy kids fishing!

In what seemed like the blink of an eye, Bill found himself in the passenger seat of Coach Kenner's 4x4 following a van filled with excited teenagers on their way north to a weekend out in nature. As the road came to an end on the scenic shore of a lake, the group made their way to their designated spot and pitched the tents. The two Kenner boys were practiced hands and got the others organized and Matt and Bill did their best to help out. Coach Kenner busied himself with the food preparation.

"You picked a great spot," Bill said when they all gathered around the fire to enjoy their hotdogs and s'mores.

"Isn't it something? We bring the team here every year for a bonding experience. I'm so glad you helped out," Coach Kenner said, "it would have been a shame to have to cancel. I'm glad Matt suggested it."

The Coach stopped abruptly as if he had said something he wasn't supposed to. Bill made a mental note. Matt suggested it? He looked over at Matt, chatting with his friends, comparing notes on the best way to start a fire on a desert island. He was a different boy from the digital ghost glued to his mobile phone.

Bill assessed the tent situation. Either he was sleeping in a 4-person tent, or he was sleeping on his own in one single tent at the end of the row. Coach Kenner caught his eye.

"You're in the little one," he said, "but it's big enough for the two of you, Matt, what do you think?"

Without a word Matt shot off to fetch their two sleeping bags, shook them open and placed them in the tent.

Bill observed how the kids followed Coach Kenner's every word, without the need to raise his voice, or make any effort. He seemed to have an aura around him, a quiet confident authority.

"I'm bushed," Bill said, "I think I'll call it a night."

"Me too," the Coach said, "Sleep well."

"That would be a first," Bill said getting up.

"Having trouble sleeping at night?"

"Yeah, I'm not big into taking pills, so..."

"Hang on a sec. This may interest you; it's actually one of our 'Upstairs' disciplines – a biblical formula on getting a good night's sleep. This worked for all of us. Just pray that when you lie down, you will not be afraid; when you lie down, your sleep will be sweet," said the coach, "Ask God for wisdom and understanding. I will explain more tomorrow." "Understanding?" Bill questioned as though he wondered what he was supposed to be trying to understand.

Coach followed quickly, "Understanding life and situations from God's perspective. Just pray as you lie down that you would be able to understand how God is working in your life. Try it." And with that, Coach walked away to check on the others.

"Amen," proclaimed Bill softly, but he wasn't so sure how sweet his sleep would be on a hard ground in a tiny tent.

Matt came in after him and settled in his sleeping bag, head to feet so they could have a little more space. They were snug, but they fit just right like two pieces in a puzzle. Bill braced himself for a long sleepless night. He said a quick prayer asking God for understanding and a good night's sleep. He remembered his conversation with Eamon earlier in the week. He made a mental list of things to be grateful for. This child next to him that meant more to him than his own life, Claire, his strong kind wife, his two beautiful daughters, Mary Anne and Amy, his business

White Tiger. He wasn't so sure that he was grateful for the business at the moment; it seemed to be nothing but a source of anxiety and trouble. This will be a long night, thought Bill. He heard muffled conversation in the other tent and the sound of the water lapping on the dock.

"Are you warm enough buddy?" Bill asked.

"Yup," said Matt, "you?"

He heard a muffled wave of giggles coming from one of the tents, then Coach Kenner's booming voice "Good night gentlemen." That was the last thing Bill remembered. When he woke up he was alone in the tent. In the bright morning sun he felt as if he had just been reborn in a fresh new body. He had slept through the night; in fact he had overslept by the look of things. The others were up and their fishing gear ready. As they later sat on the jetty, legs swinging back and forth, waiting for the fish to bite, he whispered to Coach Kenner.

"For my life, I can't believe it!" Bill said, "I slept through the entire night for the first time in years."

"Could be the fresh air," Coach Kenner said, with a knowing smile, "or that you didn't have a TV."

"Whatever Bible verse you quoted for that prayer suggestion last night," Bill said, "it worked. I don't get it though. What does wisdom and understanding have to do with sleeping well?"

"That scripture says that good sleep is the result that follows certain actions," said Coach Kenner, "*When you lie down, your sleep will be sweet.* Now, who doesn't want that?

Plus, as a bonus, we go in safety, we don't stumble, and we can lie down without fear. "It is all in *Proverbs 3:21-24 My son, do not let wisdom or understanding out of your sight, preserve sound judgment and discretion; they will be life for you, an ornament to grace your neck. Then you will go on your way in safety, and your foot will not stumble. When you lie down, you will not be afraid; when you lie down, your sleep will be sweet.*"

Their conversation was interrupted by the whooping of the boys that were reeling in something that looked like a snake and turned out to be a piece of tangled rope.

Bill had plenty to think about in the silence that followed. *Wisdom, understanding, sound judgment and discretion.* Why could it be that he found it easier to sleep in a tent than on his extra-premium mattress in a temperature-controlled room at home? Maybe because here there was nowhere to go, events were out of his control and he just had to let them roll. Maybe because he could sense his son's steady rhythmic breathing. Whatever it was, it worked. He was amazed at how just one night of sleep had cleared his head. How without exchanging almost any words, he felt closer to Matt than he had in years. Bill noticed how the kids had as much fun catching an old rope than the biggest fish in the lake. Could it be that simple? All he had to do was to hold on to this new state of mind. But Bill knew it would be far from easy or natural back home, otherwise most people would embrace these qualities. Everybody would be following healthy routines, if it were that easy. Yet most end up zoning out in front of an insane reality TV show or the football game, eating unhealthy snacks. Bill repeated his mental notes: wisdom, understanding, sound judgment, and discretion.

As the sun climbed high in the September sky the boys were squeezing every last feeling of the receding summer. They had gone for a swim and were now eating sandwiches in the shade.

"I should do this more often," Bill said to the coach, watching Matt snacking on an apple. "I want to hold on to this moment, why do we forget so easily?"

"Exactly, that's the whole point of "Upstairs" to remind each other of the disciplines," said the coach, "it keeps you from slipping back into bad habits."

"You know what you said, about wisdom, understanding, sound judgment, and discretion," Bill asked. "How do you manage to get and hold on to those?"

"Good question because those qualities are the key to a good night's sleep, man. Clear as day. First, we define

> Discipline to Get a Good Night's Sleep

them, so we know what we are seeking. We boil it down to say that *discretion* is the ability to make responsible decisions with concern and understanding of how they will impact and be received by others.

Sound judgment is the ability to discern truth and apply moral principles to make decisions. *Understanding* is the ability to see how or trust that God is working in a particular situation and *wisdom* is the ability to apply experience to all three of these in choosing a best course of action."

Bill being impressed with the deepness of the definitions rephrased his question, "Those four qualities are so life altering, how do I access them, on a daily basis?"

"Ask God to give you those things and also pray that Matt will have them too, and your wife, and your employees, and customers."

"Can I add the computer guys to the list of beneficiaries?" Bill said, pretending to write on the palm of his hand with an imaginary pen.

"I don't know Bill, that's a big ask," Coach Kenner laughed, "but seriously, can you imagine life lived with trust that God is working through all things? Certainly takes the pressure off and helps us go to bed at night without worry and stress keeping us awake!"

We need a good night's sleep for our own good health. God did not design us to live on four hours sleep. That is just not sustainable long term. Before electricity, people slept nine or ten hours per night. Now the average is seven and declining. For many business owners, much less. When we don't get enough sleep, we can be more susceptible to stress. We often pursue our business achievement dreams at a price, yet most reports still say we should get eight hours of sleep per night for maximum benefit and stress reduction to body and mind.

"Life is way too short and meaningful to be spent waking up in a sweat with worry. I encourage you to seek and hold on to wisdom, understanding, sound judgment and discretion and see for yourself the difference that makes in your life. All of us found this discipline to be essential, and it also makes a difference in how people respond to you.

You'll give off a certain reassurance to others. People will be attracted to you like you're really wearing a sign around your neck that you are dependable, steady."

"So that's your secret," Bill said, "the reason kids follow you."

Coach Kenner laughed, and then switched gears.

"I can see something in you Bill, the most important key to the whole kit and caboodle to whether or not these disciplines will make a difference in your life. Something that we all are born with but most adults kill dead."

"What's that?"

"You are open to learning. You are teachable."

CHAPTER 5

Discipline to Celebrate Progress, not Perfection

When Eamon arrived on Monday morning he was surprised to see that Bill was already up to his elbows in paperwork. He tried not to make noise as he had his breakfast and went through his daily routine of preparing a to-do list before he opened his email – he knew very well that once he opened the floodgates to external messages his brain would be too cluttered to think clearly of the priorities. When he finished, he knocked gently on Bill's open door.

"Mornin' boss," Eamon said, "Looks like you finally had a good night's sleep?"

"Can you tell?" Bill said, "It was like a miracle, in the most uncomfortable bed I've slept in for a long while, pretty much on the floor, in a tent, and I slept like an angel. Then back home, the same. I feel ten years younger. No, scratch that. It's not that I feel younger. I feel ten years... healthier."

"Answer to your prayers," Eamon said.
"Amen," nodded Bill, and they both got to the sticky task of piecing together the three brothers' billing history from hand-filled logs, bank statements and what printed invoices they had, to see if they could find the discrepancies that the customers had pointed out.

They wrapped up in two hours, with a clearer picture of where they stood.

"I'm off to my lunch appointment," Bill said, "see if you can schedule a meeting with them, the sooner the better. No need to procrastinate. Great job putting together all that stuff, Eamon. Well done."

Bill joined the other members of the Upstairs group at the diner. Bill now really looked forward to their meetings. It all felt so natural, slightly festive, like meeting friends. He realized how lucky he was to have these chats, now that Pete was no longer there to see him through the bumps on the road. There would never be a substitute for his dear best friend, but he would feel much lonelier without these random bunch of 'Upstairs' business peers. The food was delicious as usual, today there was a big slab of roast lamb that fell apart with a fork, accompanied with a Mediterranean sauce that Bill couldn't quite make out, it had mint, maybe some lemon. It was mouthwatering.

"So we heard the fishing trip was a roaring success," said Conrad, "...for the fish!"

"Yup, happy to report all the fish got away safely," said Coach Kenner as everyone laughed.

"We had a great time," said Bill, "You know what coach? My son this morning got ready for school almost like a normal human being. I mean, it still took two wake-up knocks on the door, even though the plumber had already been banging on the wall for half an hour, but still..."

"Still.... its progress, right?" said Coach Kenner.

> Discipline to Celebrate Progress, Not Perfection

"Progress?" said Bill, "yes, not perfect. But definitely progress."

"You hit the nail on the head, Bill. Progress, not perfection," said the coach, "Does that remind you of something Diane?"

"That is such an important discipline," Diane said, "celebrating progress, not perfection. It's key to reducing or eliminating stress in our life to make sure that we are measuring or viewing our life correctly."

"Why don't you share your story, Diane, I think Bill may find it interesting," Conrad said.

"This sounds so simple, but for me, for all of us, it brought clarity. Just on any average day a little thing happens that shines a light on a new understanding of what is really important. I had one of those moments not very long ago. You know, of all the things that can keep you up at night, for me it was my son's baseball games. After my husband passed, I was so intensely focused on my son not missing out on any experiences that I went to every single game. He's thirteen and quite good. He made the all-star team, actually, and got to play in the Dizzy Dean World Series.

So on one day it was quite a crucial game, an elimination game, he was up to bat against one of the best pitchers in the entire tournament. I remember as if I could see him right now. The pitcher was a left-hander with a good fastball and great curveball. My son was down in the count with two strikes and no balls. It didn't look good. I remember thinking and hoping that he would not strike out. Then all of a sudden, on the next pitch, he just crushed it. In the stands, we all jumped to our feet and watched as the ball seemed to go a mile high and it looked like it was going over the homerun fence.

However, the ball hit the fence about five inches short of going over. My heart dropped. I couldn't believe it. So close to a home run and it just barely fell short. I could hear the voice in my head: he really got under it too much. If his swing had been more level, the ball would have been long gone. My thoughts were already racing ahead, I was thinking about how I could hire someone to help him work on his swing. There I was, thinking about what could have been rather than celebrating the fact that my son had hit a double. Then I saw something that took my breath away. On second base, my son was celebrating with his arms stretched up in the air. He looked blissfully happy, big white-toothed grin, completely in the moment. His teammates were cheering and going crazy. I realized that I had managed to make myself unhappy by measuring his performance against a supposedly perfect outcome. Then it hit me, clear as day, if I only celebrated perfection I would be hard pressed to find any reason to celebrate at all, ever, anything, seeing as we live in an imperfect world."

"When Diane shared this with us it immediately made sense," Conrad said, "we could all relate. We were all doing it at work, at home, and most of all with ourselves!"

"I know exactly what you mean," said Bill, "when we were out fishing, the kids thought they had caught something big, but it was only a piece of old rope. I was disappointed for them, but what you said right now made me realize that the kids were laughing at their fishing misadventures and having a great time. I'm so glad I didn't say anything that day and didn't spoil the moment. The whole point was not the size of the fish, but being together and making these funny memories!"

"Precisely," said Conrad, "and now you have to be careful about something, we must warn you. You'll start making a mental inventory of all the beautiful moments you missed because you were obsessed with perfection instead of progress. Don't look back. Look forward. We're all guilty of missing lots of opportunities and probably put a lot of unnecessary stress on our life by always thinking about what could have been, rather than simply celebrating what happened. I regret the times that I did not praise my kids for doing their best, even when they didn't win. Certainly, I have gotten better over time at this and really now see myself as an appreciator of life. It has allowed me to appreciate how God is working in my life, my family's life, and in the business."

"I still strive for perfection, mind you," said Diane, "but the difference is that I know that it's not likely to happen and I do not measure myself against the 'perfection yardstick' anymore. That has been a huge stress reduction for me. As I reflect back, much of the stress that I have had in life has been self-inflicted."

Bill left the lunch energized and ready to take the bull by the horns. Eamon had texted him from the office that the three brothers were available for a brief meeting if he could make it by 2pm. Bill headed straight for the medical offices. Just two of the brothers were there, but Bill could already sense that their body language had softened slightly, just by the mere fact that he had taken the initiative to come and see them.

Bill went over what he and Eamon had found that morning. There was one billing mistake, probably as a result of the change of invoice system, and one mistake on the logs. He offered compensation as a refund or he would double the amount as future credit if they decided to stay on as his customers, but that he totally understood if they preferred to take their business elsewhere.

"Of course if we find any further mistakes when we have access to the billing system we'll compensate you accordingly," Bill said, "but there doesn't seem to have been any ill will or deliberate act, just a combination of independent random errors..."

The brothers thanked Bill again for his visit and said they would talk to the third brother that was not present at the meeting and let Bill know by the end of the week.

"It's great to see that you took our complaint seriously," said one of the brothers.

"Of course!" Bill said, "You've been loyal clients for years, and that means a lot to me."

On his way back to the office Bill reflected on what Diane had said during lunch, about celebrating progress. As a business owner it was so easy to be consumed by the upsets. He used to take it very hard when an employee would quit, or as in the case of the three brothers, a huge misunderstanding with a customer. It is easy to take it personal and feel wronged and let down. But Bill now realized that he had a choice, and during the meeting with the three brothers instead of taking a confrontational or defensive stance he had chosen to be thankful for the business they had given him so far.

Bill's mind kept going back in particular to what Diane said about most of her stress being self-inflicted. Those words had been a revelation. That must have been a difficult thing for Diane to admit, and he was so glad that she had shared that story with him.

Bill thought he could dwell on the software mishap that had brought White Tiger to its knees, but instead he chose to focus on what a great job Eamon had done digging up the information manually to keep things going until the software issues could be worked out. While he could not ignore the impact of the setbacks, he had a choice to direct his attention to the baby steps that led towards a possible solution.

Bill thought back to what coach Kenner said to him about being 'teachable'. He was right. As an entrepreneur, mostly self-taught on the job, what Bill enjoyed most was learning. So these great disciplines he was learning from the Upstairs group, each one of them was a step towards stressing less in his business. While the mastery of the disciplines he had learned so far was far from perfect, he decided to focus on the progress he was making. Not just related strictly to his job. He was sleeping better, eating better, and walking more. His head felt clearer. Maybe there were other people out there who would not be open to learning the disciplines and would discard them before giving them a chance. This is probably why Coach Kenner liked what he saw in him. The thought of being teachable gave Bill great comfort.

"So?" Eamon said as Bill arrived at the White Tiger office, "no black eyes?"

"Better than could be expected," Bill said, "we should hear back from them by the end of the week."

"You think they'll take the offer of credit and stay with us?" Eamon said, "They sounded so angry before."

"Too early to tell," said Bill, "but right now I am grateful for at least three things."

"Really? What's that?" Eamon said.

"First, that we didn't let the situation escalate, and we had a civilized conversation. Second, that our cleaners hadn't lied to us and it was all an honest mistake, and third, but most importantly, for the great job you did straightening out the paperwork."

"Oh, I don't know about that boss, it was far from perfect."

"It wasn't perfection, it was better than that... it was progress," Bill said, smiling to himself.

"Guess what, boss, I'll give you a fourth thing to be thankful for. Maybe you need to sit down for this one."

"It couldn't be..."

Eamon slowly nodded towards the back of the office, where Bill now noticed the back of two heads surrounded by four laptops and a mass of cables. The software guys.

"How did you rope them in?" Bill whispered.

"They just showed up, right after you left."

"Just like that? Did they say if they found the glitch?" Eamon shrugged, "No, they didn't say much, they just asked if they could set up and start working, so I said yes."

"Whatever the result," Bill said, "they're here, and that's definitely progress."

"There's something different about you, boss," said Eamon, raising his eyebrows. "This sleeping through the night business really agrees with you."

"Do you think I should talk to them?" Bill said.

"No, it's like the sighting of a rare species in the wild," Eamon said, imitating a documentary narrator,

"...better to observe them from a distance, undisturbed."

--

Arriving home before sundown had become a rare occurrence. Bill retrieved the package from the back of his car, with the commotion about the hospital scare and then the fishing trip he had completely forgotten to give Claire the replacement crystal bowl. Bill surveyed the entrance hall and was pleasantly surprised to see that the wall was whole again, even though just the rough plasterboard was up and the contents of the room were still boxed up. Most of the dust was gone. Claire's car wasn't in the driveway, she must have had gone out to the store. He left the gift on the kitchen table so Claire could see it as soon as she got back. He should have gotten her flowers. He'd get some tomorrow. Claire loved flowers. Matt was alone in the backyard, airing the camping gear to store it back in the garage.

"Need a hand?" Bill said, grabbing the other sleeping bag and starting to fold it.

As they were done and Bill reached over to switch off the garage light, he turned to Matt and quickly said, "by the way, I meant to tell you this morning, good job getting up a little faster. I know you find it hard, and I appreciate it. Made my morning much easier."

Matt didn't say anything and climbed back upstairs. A few minutes later Bill could hear Matt singing out loud to one of his favorite tracks in his room. Bill made a mental note. *That's the sound of progress.*

Bill looked back to the day. Just in these past twelve hours he had so much to be thankful for. It was really quite amazing how much he could add to his gratitude list. He had a positive meeting with a client, he had improved his communication with his son, he had met with colleagues and learned a valuable discipline from them. While at the end of the day Bill usually felt drained, logging these successes in his mind made him feel less tired. The more he documented progress and added things to the mental list, the more things he seemed to notice and remember, all the good things that had happened in the last few days. He had a health scare, but the doctors found everything was alright. The fishing trip had given him new memories to cherish, spending time with his son.

Bill decided he'd call Mary Anne and Amy and see if they'd come over for a weekend. He still hadn't quite gotten used to them both being away at college. He had been meaning to call his daughters; it had been a few weeks since their last visit. That would make Claire happy, and Matt too even though he would never admit out loud to missing his sisters.

Bill was thankful for Diane, for sharing with him her story of her son's baseball game and helping him realize that a large part of his unhappiness was of his own doing. From this day forward, Bill would celebrate progress. He knew that even if any future 'big fish' turned out to be a piece of old rope, he would be okay. He could accept that. The world would not come to an end. Perfection was no longer his measuring yardstick.

Then he noticed the note on his night table. It was from Claire.

CHAPTER 6

Discipline to Learn from Mistakes
and not Dwell on Them

Holding Claire's letter in his hands, Bill felt his arms become heavy as if the thin delicate paper weighed too much for him to hold up. He could understand the words, but couldn't follow the meaning. He knew things weren't perfect, but where was this coming from?

If you have made a mistake, tell me. What hurts me the most is the feeling that you can't talk to me and you need to hide. Please reflect on the promises you made, and what they mean... and the effect of your actions on the people who love you.

-Claire

What hit Bill the hardest was not so much the content of the message but the fact that Claire had signed her name. Usually on their everyday notes or little reminders she would sign a C preceded by a heart. Seeing her formal name made him feel miles away from her. What could this refer to; he had made so many mistakes! He knew he hadn't been as present as he should have been. Most of the past few months had been taken over by preoccupations with work and feeling sorry for himself, his health, and missing his friend Pete. Bill couldn't think of one thing that could have triggered such a message; it was so unlike Claire. Just when things had started to slightly straighten out at White Tiger, something goes off the rails at home. He better call Claire right away.

Just then Bill heard two familiar voices calling out from the kitchen, "Dad! Mom! You guys! Surprise!"
The voices of his two daughters Mary Anne and Amy lifted Bill's heart like heavenly music. If he had spotted a life raft after a shipwreck, he could not have felt more relieved. He rushed down the stairs and swept his two lovely daughters in his arms at once.

"We brought Greek food!" said Amy, lifting the bags onto the kitchen table, "from the diner on the boardwalk. Wait till you try it. It's amazing."

"You know about that diner?" said Bill.

"Oh, yeah!" said Mary Anne, ruffling Matt's hair, "it was this little guy here that told us about it!"

Matt looked away, pretending he hadn't heard. Was he avoiding Bill's eyes?

"Does Mom know you're home?" Bill asked.

"No, we thought we'd surprise you guys, Amy has an interview for an internship tomorrow and I tagged along to share the drive. Where's Mom?"

"Err...Why don't you call her?" Bill said, avoiding the question, "she'll be so happy!"

Bill thought it might be a bit cowardly to use his daughters to reach out to Claire. It wasn't clear from her note when, or even if, she was to be home. Isn't that one of family's sweetest functions after all? To help us climb out of the unwitting holes we dig for ourselves?

When Claire arrived, the table was set, Mary Anne and Amy had kept dinner warm in the oven and Matt was finishing his homework upstairs. Bill went out to greet her as he helped with some groceries from the back of the car.

"The girls are here!" Bill said.

"I know, they called me."

"Can we talk for a second about the note?"

"Not now," Claire said, "let's talk after dinner when the kids go upstairs."

The kids. It was automatic, although Mary Anne and Amy were now beautiful young women, it was impossible to adjust to their 'grown up' status in their parents' hearts. As soon as Claire had said hello to the girls, her eyes went to the gift-wrapped package that Bill had left for her on the table. She naturally assumed it was from the girls. She opened it and admired the beautiful crystal fruit bowl, then looked at her daughters.

"How did you know?" she said.

"What?" Mary Anne asked.

"That my favorite bowl broke," Claire said.

Amy hesitated, "It's not from us."

Claire blinked rapidly as if trying to understand. Then she looked at Bill.

"Do you like it?" he said, with a fixed smile worthy of a toothpaste commercial.

Claire didn't reply, as if he was speaking in a language she couldn't understand. She set the bowl carefully on the upper shelf where the old one had been on display. It reflected light from the overhead fixture and created tiny little rainbows on the ceiling. Claire had a magical touch for making their home beautiful. Even during their most frugal years, when Bill was starting the business, she could make the simplest details look much more upscale than their hand-me-downs could ever hope for. Bill noticed that Claire's hands were slightly shaking. Whatever had upset her, she felt it deeply. Nothing could be further away from his intentions than to cause her distress. He could not forgive himself if anything he had done had affected her in this way. He ached to protect her, to reassure her, but she was miles and miles away, unreachable in her unease. He attempted a timid approach.

"I'm sorry I didn't give it to you right away, I've had it for days, I had my little hospital scare that day, and then I just..."

Claire's eyes were even more watery than usual. Was she sad? Angry? Bill could not read her expression. Their conversation would have to wait as talk quickly turned to Bill's health. The girls wanted to be reassured that there was no reason for concern.

"I'm perfectly fine," Bill said, "nothing to worry about. I was just a little stressed."

"You know, Dad," said Amy, "you really have to be careful about stress. I read an article in a magazine that a study showed that relentless stress can damage people's immune system and speed up the aging process."

"I agree," Mary Anne jumped on board, "medical studies have proven prolonged stress can cause all kinds of problems, high blood pressure, heart disease, depression, diabetes and even weight disorders and memory loss. There really is no good reason to let stress control your life."

"Oh, I don't think you two have to worry about aging quite yet! But I'm glad to know you both have found ways to deal with stress. I'm working on some disciplines," Bill said, "in fact, I am making great progress."

Matt shot a sideways glance at Bill. Or was Bill imagining things?

When the food came out, everyone commented on the delicious braised lamb with a light mint sauce and the accompanying potato salad with a creamy tzatziki dressing. It was indeed remarkable. Bill recognized the dish from one of the Upstairs group lunches.

"So you knew about the food from this diner, huh?" Bill asked Matt.

Matt nodded, filling his mouth with another forkful so he wouldn't have to speak. Bill was now sure there was something Matt was holding back. It felt as if he was about to start to say something and then decided not to.

"I've had lunch there myself a few times," Bill said, "with Conrad and a group of business owners that meet to talk about how to manage stress in our work life."

Bill went on to briefly describe the disciplines he had learned and how they were already helping him. Mary Anne and Amy showed a particular interest, but Claire seemed to be reserving judgment. Bill realized that he hadn't talked to Claire about his meetings with the group, and it made him wonder why. What was it that had made him clam up recently? He used to share every single detail of his day with Claire, and they always found some way to laugh about the little annoyances of dealing with a growing business, and they would quickly become running jokes, like a private shorthand they shared. He tried to revive that feeling of easy communication and make light of things.

"You know what's funny, they call these meetings 'Upstairs'!"

Claire was taking a sip from her glass of water, and stopped with the glass mid-air.

"Upstairs," she repeated, as if learning a new foreign word.

"Yes, Upstairs!" Bill said, "It had me going the first time, I thought that it was actually a meeting in a room on the second floor. But the name refers to the fact that there's a 'higher purpose' to our business, that honors and serves the Lord, and these meetings serve to remind us of that purpose, in contrast to the 'downstairs' mundane material aspects that tend to command most of our attention and cause a lot of stress."

"That makes sense to me," Amy said, "how did you find these people, Dad?"

"Conrad approached me at Pete's funeral," Bill said.

"How sensitive of him," Mary Anne tilted her head, "to realize you needed to talk to someone."

"It's amazing," Bill said, "he knew that I needed it before I even did. At first I didn't even want to go to these meetings. I felt sooooo awkward."

Bill looked over at Matt and Claire and they both had an odd expression on their faces. Mary Anne had a way of always directly cutting to the heart of any issues within the family. She did it again.

"OK, Mom, Matt, you're both freaking me out," she said, "what's up?"

"Nothing," Matt said, resorting back to his usual shrug.

"Come on Matt," said Mary Anne, "You're both acting like you've seen a ghost."

Claire was starting to say something when Matt interrupted.

"It was me..." he said, almost too low to be heard.

"What was?" Bill leaned in with his eyebrows raised.

"I asked Mr. Conrad," Matt said.

"You asked him what?"

"We started talking," Matt said, "when I was volunteering for the church hall, Mr. Green would bring food from the diner for all the volunteers, trying different Greek recipes and asking us if we liked it better this way or that... anyway... one day he was talking to Mr. Conrad and Coach Kenner was there too, and they mentioned they were on their way to their lunch. Mr. Conrad said to send his regards and asked me how you were doing. So I said that I was worried that you would get sick from stressing about the business. He offered to talk to you, if that was okay with me. Then that day at the cemetery you looked so... so..." Matt shrugged again. "I asked him to go talk to you. It was me."

Bill didn't know what to say. He was touched that Matt was worried about him, and at the same time wounded that his son had seen it fit to discuss this with someone else before talking to him. Just then, Claire got up from her chair without saying a word, her eyes brimming with tears, and went out through the glass doors and kept walking rapidly to the bottom of the garden until she was almost out of sight. Dusk was settling in and the garden lights were coming on, reflecting on the limpid swimming pool. This was when the house looked at its most beautiful. Claire's beautiful garden at twilight. Yet today the beauty was lost on Bill, his heart heavy with Matt's revelations and Claire's distress. He stopped just a few feet away from where Claire was sitting on a low garden wall, facing away from the house.

"It's not a big deal, really" Bill said, "Matt had his heart in the right place, he meant well, I'll talk to him later."

Claire shook her head. Was she crying?

"Honestly, I don't mind," he said, "It was a blessing to find those people just when I needed them. Matt had the right instinct, I did need to talk to someone."

Claire's shoulders slightly quivered up and down as she tried to speak through brimming tears.

"I'm so sorry," she said, "that horrible note."

The only words he could make out from what followed from Claire were "phone" "message" "upstairs", then "a gift", "receipt". Suddenly it clicked. Claire had seen Conrad's message on his phone to meet 'upstairs', she had seen the credit card payment with the purchase from her favorite store, but hadn't yet received any gift. Then him staying late so often at work... it all added up to a shadowy picture.

"You thought I was having an affair?" Bill asked, laughing out loud with pure relief.

"I didn't know what to think," Claire said, "it was all so confusing."

She was now laughing through her tears as Bill held her in his arms, "You silly goose! Why didn't you ask me?"

"And you? Why didn't you tell me about the meetings? I would have liked to thank Conrad personally."

"I don't know. It's not that I didn't feel I could come to you. I think maybe I didn't want to admit to myself, you know, that I was sinking, that I was in trouble. I always want to be the one to fix things, and now I was the one that needed fixing."

"We need to tell each other what's going on," Claire said, "like we used to. We can't ask Matt to communicate with us if we don't set an example."

"Absolutely," Bill said, "open lines starting now."

"Maybe not tell Matt the part about thinking you were messing around..." Claire smiled and her eyes turned back to blue.

"OK maybe we'll skip that part..." he said, kissing the top of her head. He then noticed the lighting on the pool, the last fading reflection of the sun on the climbing roses.

Through the French doors they could see Mary Anne, Amy and Matt clearing the table and tidying up the kitchen. Amy was doing her funny dance trying to make Matt laugh, and it was working.

"Doesn't our house look beautiful?"

--

During lunch with the Upstairs group that week, Bill recounted the story, including the comic turn it took with Claire's misunderstanding of Bill's alleged escapades.

"We couldn't stop laughing," Bill said, "but then afterwards I kept having these flashbacks thinking of what unnecessary pain I have inflicted on my family, having my twelve-year-old son worry about me so much, and my wife in tears, my two older daughters concerned about my health. It's frightening. As if I had a constant voice in my head torturing me, saying that I can't relax because it can all just spiral out of control so quickly."

"That voice in your head is not you," said Ted, one of the quietest members of the group who had a slight speech impediment after recovering from a stroke years ago. "I know from experience."

"Do you mean the discipline to learn from mistakes and not dwell on them?" Diane said.

Ted nodded. Bill wanted to know more, but he didn't want to push him into sharing something personal if he wasn't ready. Ted reached out for the salad, helped himself and passed it around. There was silence at the table, as if allowing the space necessary for Ted's story to walk out on stage.

"Forgive me if this sounds a bit strange to you," Ted said, "we all hear the same voice."

Ted rounded up each word carefully, arching his eyebrows now and then in a sort of punctuation, as if to confirm the listener was following.

"The voice in our head that reminds us of our past and wants us to dwell on our faults and mistakes is not us, its Satan pulling us down and trying to rob us of our joy. Jesus is concerned with our present and future purpose, lifting us up. While a few fortunate people never have this problem, for most of us - all of us in this case - we can get stuck in the mire."

Ted's speech was now becoming more fluid, as if it was an engine that had just needed warming up. His cheeks were slightly flushed.

Bill felt uneasy, he felt the urge to get up and leave right then and there. What was this kind of talk among business people? It sounded obscure, impenetrable. He didn't want Ted to continue, he didn't want to hear any more of this story.

"This is an uncomfortable thing to accept," Ted said, as if he sensed Bill's unease, "we don't want to think that we have Satan's voice inside our heads. It's that denial that gives him the advantage."

Bill started to quickly run through his head the possible excuses he could make up for getting up and rushing away from the table.

"He wants us to focus and dwell on our past, especially bad decisions and

Discipline to Learn from Mistakes and Not Dwell on Them

mistakes," Ted continued. "However, focusing on mistakes often creates feelings of regret, frustration or even anger, which are stress triggers. For me it had gotten so bad that it was a constant running commentary, day and night to the point that I ended up one fine morning in the emergency room with the left side of me completely paralyzed. It was like being locked up with a caged animal, even though I couldn't speak or move, the voice would not stop. I remember looking up at the bright overhead light in the hospital and decided, right there, that if I made it out of that hospital bed, I would never ever allow myself to listen to that voice again. Thanks to the care of a wonderful team of doctors and nurses and my loving wife, I pulled through. I kept my promise and never listened to Satan again. I can't tell you how much my life improved. If the stroke was the price to pay for this kind of awareness, then I'll take it."

"I'm so happy to see that you recovered so incredibly well," Bill said.

"I was fortunate, there's practically no trace, I just slur my lines here and there... but you're even luckier because you can take this from me, you don't need to have a stroke to find out!" Ted smiled with a grin that lit up his entire face.

"So how do you keep from falling into the trap again?" Bill asked.

"It's not easy. We talk about it here, of course, as one of our disciplines. It's one that comes up very often. It's a choice. A decision you make. As soon as you catch yourself talking about or thinking about a negative past situation, you must choose to stop. If your spouse or a friend or co-worker starts to stir up a bucket of negative thoughts, simply say that you don't want to talk about that, and that you prefer to focus on what you learned from it and move on. Likewise, if they say the same to you, respect it."

"How do I know that it's Satan, and not my own voice warning me of not making the same mistake twice?" Bill said.

"That's a great question," Ted said, "notice that we didn't call the discipline ignore your mistakes or forget the mistakes. We call it 'learn' from your mistakes. Just don't dwell on them. Have you ever noticed that when you try not to think about something, that's all you're actually thinking about? Don't get stuck in that pattern. Incorporate the lesson, brand it into your mind with fire if you must – just don't let the fire consume you. Life is too short to dwell on past mistakes and we certainly don't need the added stress."

"In my experience, one thing I noticed," Diane said, "is that when I started to learn from my mistakes, I would forget some things and remember the important parts. It made me wonder if my brain was able to choose what to retain and what to discard, that if I could ask God to 'filter' my brain and allow me to 'forget' those things that were holding me back. I don't know why it never occurred to me earlier, to turn my memories over to God?"

"Exactly. Here's the thing, Bill," Ted said, "I could have gotten stuck and you wouldn't have blamed me. I could have kept going 'if only' for my stroke, if only I hadn't driven my body so hard, if only I had eaten better, exercised, gotten more sleep. But you'll agree with me that what's important is what I do now, from now on, this moment, with you, right here. No amount of worrying will change the past. If you find yourself wanting to 'live' in the past, and not move forward, ask God to remove those dwelling thoughts from your memory and replace them with constructive thoughts or the memories of the lessons you learned."

There were collective nods of agreement all around the table. It made Bill think that maybe Ted wasn't losing his marbles after all. Could he be on to something here?

As if he was reading his mind, Ted said, "You may be wondering what all of this self- taught psychology has to do with business success or living a stress less work life."

Bill nodded, with a slightly guilty half-grin.

"This is all I have to say: try it and find out for yourself," and with that Ted went back to concentrating on his food and spoke no more.

Conrad took over the conversation, sensing that Bill was still seeking validation to digest this discipline.

"I remember when Ted first told us about this discipline that he discovered while he was in the hospital," Conrad said. "We were all finding it difficult to accept that it was so easy, that you could decide and choose overnight not to listen to that voice again, to not dwell on the negative. Then it occurred to me, what if that doubt was coming from precisely that same voice, sabotaging our efforts. So I tried to silence it. It works. While there are some stressors or events we cannot control, our negative thinking about the past is one stressor we can control with conscious awareness and discipline."

"Can you think of one person who has never made a mistake?" asked Diane.

Bill started to see the point. Of course he couldn't. Everybody makes mistakes.

"Mistakes are part of the human experience," she continued, "If we categorize them as 'learning', we can see how they actually contribute to wisdom. Since we are to seek wisdom, according to scripture, it is fair to say that learning from mistakes can become part of that process. Coach Kenner here could write a book about it."

The coach laughed in agreement.

"I certainly could write at least the Wikipedia page," he said, "I have taught for many years to view mistakes as part of the process of getting better. I just say to the kids to try to learn from these lessons the first time, if possible during practice, for the sake of the team, so they don't have to repeat the same mistake again during an important game."

"See Bill? Even the great coach likes mistakes. The beauty of these meetings is that we can all learn from each other and keep reminding ourselves to learn and move forward. Plus it saves us time, money and stress." said Diane.

"It could even save our businesses." Conrad added.

CHAPTER 7

Discipline to Invest in Quality
and Loving Relationships

On his way to work the next morning, Bill offered Amy a lift to her internship interview. She entered the address on the navigation system and Bill just followed directions.

"How are you feeling about the interview honey?"

"Great!" Amy cheerfully replied with confidence, "it's an amazing place, these guys are among the top in the whole country, and they are so close to home."

"I hope you'll live at home while you're there?"

"First I have to get it, Dad!" she laughed, "though I appreciate the confidence."

"They'd be lucky to have you." Bill made clear his proud father position.

To everyone's surprise Amy had chosen to become a dental lab technician. She was always very skilled at making things, and very interested in computers and 3D modeling. There was no one in the family or friends with that profession and so they assumed that it must have made an impression when she went in to the dentist as a child. It's funny how these things work out, Bill was thinking, as he suddenly felt a certain déjà vu, although he didn't know why. He understood the feeling of having been here before as soon as they reached their destination and Bill found himself turning into the parking lot of the offices of the three brothers. You've got to be kidding.

"You OK Dad?" Amy asked.

"Sure, I'm just running a little late for work so I'll drop you off quickly if you don't mind."
Amy quickly opened the door, "No worries, and thanks for the ride!"

"Good luck honey, you're going to be great!" he called out as he drove off.

Bill felt relieved that he had never been rude or blown his top during the talks or emails with the three brothers. Even though he had been visibly flustered, he had kept his composure and so had Eamon. If things had gotten heated, he would have had to warn Amy, as the three brothers would likely make the connection and know who her father was. Goes to show, Bill thought, you never know.

As he arrived in the office, Eamon was already busy shuttling between the computer and the printer. He was collating several copies of the same file on his desk, and then going back to his computer to print the next batch.

"Mornin' boss!" Eamon said, "You've got some good news coming."

"Really?"

"Yes, I think I found the jinx in the accounts. Give me another 15 minutes and I'll have it ready."

It took Eamon a little longer, more like thirty minutes to get the paperwork ready. He gave a copy to Bill and kept one for himself.

"I spoke with our cleaners again," Eamon said, "I think the miscommunication happened with a change of shifts, if you look at July 30, they marked the extra service as done, but it was not invoiced."

Bill found the page and nodded.

"OK, here's what happened, this day for example one of the doctors at the three brothers was working later than usual, he asked our guys if they could stop the noise for the evening. But they had already checked the extra service on the log, and if you look back here, it was invoiced."

Eamon pointed out three more discrepancies.

"Finally right here, the extra service is not logged as done, and is not invoiced, but they did carry out the work. They compensated."

"So we invoiced for something we didn't do, and then didn't invoice for doing it later?" Bill said.

"Exactly," Eamon said, "but we were changing over to the new software and started having problems. Otherwise these wouldn't match and we would have corrected it. So it's nobody's fault really, just a combination of factors. We are just now figuring this out."

"Don't you think it's a bit over the top for them to react like this over an invoice though?"

"Well, here's the thing. As Murphy's Law would have it, the three brothers had a serious concern with missing medication from their secure storage, the kind of thing you need to report to the authorities," Eamon said. "It was completely unrelated to us, but it happened at the same time. They were in a bit of a firestorm and under a lot of stress. Then with our computer glitches and another miscue in service, it just added fuel to the fire."

"So they thought we were taking advantage of them?"

"I don't know, maybe," Eamon said, "better not to assume and talk to them directly and clear the air."

"You think?" Bill said, and told Eamon about the incredible coincidence of Amy's internship.

"So she may actually be working at the three brother's offices?" Eamon asked, as if thinking out loud.

"How about that," Bill shook his head in amazement.

"It's a small world... but I wouldn't want to clean it."

"Is that one of your Irish sayings?"

"No, that's an Eamon original."

Eamon always made Bill laugh, and humor was such a precious thing to share in a work relationship. In any relationship really. Having a colleague or employee you can trust, who'll be there when the potatoes get too hot to handle, and will make you smile just at the right time before your stress runs away from you. That is indeed something to treasure.

"So I'm guessing I'll call the three brothers and ask them when you can come by?" Eamon said.

"That would be great. Well done on finding the glitch, Eamon, I appreciate it."

At lunchtime, on his way to the Upstairs meeting at the diner, Bill was still thinking about Eamon, and how relationships come in all shapes and forms. How important a good work relationship is to our wellbeing? He wondered if Eamon knew how much he valued his work and his... could he call it friendship. Yes, it certainly was a friendship. They had never been to each other's homes, or even shared a proper meal together, besides the breakfasts or takeaway lunches in the office. They probably would never watch a game or go bowling, but there was certainly a mutual understanding, and a deep appreciation for each other. They had a professional friendship.

--

Today the table of the Upstairs lunch was full to capacity; Bill counted twelve guests including himself. He felt comfortable among them, as if they were family, and thought again about how important these lunch meetings had become. If he had to classify these relationships under a label, he would probably say they would fall under 'networking', but in reality it was so much more than that. He had shared with his peers situations and challenges that only they could relate to on the same level, as fellow business owners.

They had given him a fresh perspective that potentially improved his health, his business and, incidentally, his marriage, or at least brought it back from the brink of an irreparable fracture. He thought he should say something to them, to express how much he valued their input and he appreciated their sharing their experiences with him. He found his moment during a lull in the conversation, just before dessert.

"You know, I just wanted to say to you guys that I really appreciate your sharing your business and personal experiences with me," Bill said. "It came to my attention very recently that the reason I am here at all is that my son asked Conrad if he could talk to me."

Conrad looked up with his hands filled with a stack of dessert plates he had been helping pass around. He met Bill's eyes with the plate's mid-air, until Diane, who was sitting to his right, took the plates from his hands and set them down.

"He did," Conrad said, "and I am so relieved that he told you. He said he was worried about you, and I thought our little get-togethers could help you as they have helped me and all of us all these years. I hope you don't mind. I didn't mean to invade your privacy but I didn't want to betray his confidence. Such a smart and caring young man."

"Of course I don't mind," Bill said, "normally I would, but you guys have taught me a great deal. Everything suddenly seems so connected around me, where just a few months ago I felt like an island, no, not like an island that would be easier. I felt like one of those icebreakers, you know, the exploration ships with a reinforced hull. I felt as if any forward progress was just up to me, under my own power, and I was alone to break through the resistance of what was ahead. And I tell you, my ship was stuck. I believe if I had remained in that place the ice around me would have continued to build its pressure until it crushed me."

"That's a great analogy," Diane said, "that is such a good way to describe the way I felt after my husband Frank died. He had been the social focus of our lives; he was the friend- maker, the problem-solver, the party-organizer. Without him I felt everything harden, isolating me inside. What I found out when I shared my experience here is that you don't really need to be widowed or single or in a rocky marriage to feel this way. You can feel isolated and out of reach even if you are surrounded by people."

Bill was amazed at how perceptive Diane was.

"Don't tell me there's a discipline about this," Bill said, half-joking, half-hoping that there was an insight to be learned about such a critical aspect of his life.

"Of course!" Coach Kenner said in his particular booming voice, "How did you guess? And to sweeten the lesson, here comes the most excellent strawberry tartlets you'll ever have the luck of biting into..."

He was right. It was a picture of luscious red berries arranged in tidy slices around a creamy center, set on a bed of pastry light as a cloud that flaked apart with the slightest pressure from the spoon.

"I can't believe this food just keeps getting more and more delicious," Bill said.

"This is a world class establishment," Syd winked.

A sense of wellbeing washed over Bill. It could be the great food, or the good company, or the fact that danger had been averted at White Tiger and his business seemed to be getting back on track, or that he had cleared the air with Claire. This was probably the most important factor of them all. If he had Claire on his side, as he always had, he felt as if he could face anything that life threw at him.

"Go ahead, Diane," said Syd, tucking in his own pastry creation with gusto, "we are ready."

> # Discipline to Invest in Quality and Loving Relationships

"Good relationships are critical to living with less stress," said Diane, "so we call this the discipline to invest in quality and loving relationships, and this is especially true for married people, as it relates to a relationship with their spouse. Single people sometimes idealize the dream of a happy marriage, but of course, the reality we find out later on is that a rocky marriage can create a lot of stress.

Few people know this, but my marriage with Frank was close to the brink. We came very close to filing for divorce. We discussed it, and talked and talked, we went to marriage counseling, and spoke with our pastor. Now that I know how few years Frank had left, before cancer took him away from me, I realize even more how important every day was and feel very fortunate that we managed to find our way back to our mutual love and affection, as we spent those days together."

"So how did you manage to break the stalemate?" Bill asked.

"It was a simple comment, made to Frank in passing by our pastor, almost as a joke. He asked Frank: if you were to propose to Diane today, would she say yes?"

Bill swallowed hard. He had never thought about it that way. He had thought of marriage as a one-time transaction, not as a day-by-day commitment that needs to be rebooted. He was amazed that this lesson unexpectedly came from Diane, who was a woman who is for all intents and purposes, single.

"So, Bill, if you proposed to your wife today, would she say yes?" Diane continued, "Oh, and then another thing he said to us was that to improve our relationships, all that most of us need to do is to simplify! He said the shortest bridge between despair and hope is often a good, 'Thank you, Jesus!' and that shook us to the core. We were so locked into being right, and proving the other wrong, and bearing grudges and refusing to give ground on the most insignificant things. So insignificant that we couldn't even remember what we used to argue about. Our key to change was being able to shift from being right to being thankful."

"That's a sobering thought," acknowledged Bill, "I don't know that I would risk asking my wife's hand in marriage quite right now."

"Hey, you're not alone," Syd jumped in, "before we started working on this discipline, the relationship with my wife was quite strained. Particularly difficult because we both work together here in the diner. But we worked it out, and continue to work it out every day, and I am quite confident that if I asked her to marry me today the answer would be yes. That, Bill, fills my heart with happiness, and I feel grateful, and more than a little proud of myself, that I am able to keep my promise to her, to make her happy and to love her for better or for worse."

"Our marriage counseling sessions have tremendously helped," said Diane, "the counselor was recommended by our pastor because of his approach. He gave us lots of tips and of course different things work for different people, but the four that stick out are these."

Bill was so engrossed in this conversation that he actually reached out for a pen and wrote the four tips on a napkin.

1. Meet with God every day to talk about your spouse's needs.

2. Set aside quality time with your spouse. It doesn't have to be formal or expensive, it could be anything from date night to just walking around the block together holding hands.

3. Focus more on the areas you need to work on rather than what your spouse needs to work on.

4. Use love, serving, unselfishness, sacrifice and protection as decision filters in your marriage actions. This is how we want our spouse to describe us.

"That is a lot to chew on," said Conrad, "but you'll find that when you get started, it feels so natural and makes a lot of sense. But one thing you must know is that all these don't just happen by themselves. Diane will tell you that there is one critical ingredient that makes this all come together."

"That's right, the secret ingredient," Diane said, "and this works for any relationship, not just for married people. It works for neighbors, friends, church members, co-workers, and all people who can help each other and be there during stressful times. But first the coach needs to tell you about sharks."

"Sharks?" said Bill, looking at what he had just written down on the napkin. Sharks. Seriously?

"Oh, yeah," Coach Kenner said, as if suddenly he remembered some crucial element of the story. "You may know about this. This is something I always tell my team. You see, most sharks are unable to control their own body temperature through their metabolism. This limits their movements because they have to stay within a certain water temperature. The Great White however can somewhat regulate its body temperature. This makes it a highly efficient hunter, because it can cover a much wider area. The reason it can do this is that it has a network of blood vessels between its swimming muscles called a rete mirabile, a 'miracle network'. This rete mirabile is so efficient that hardly any body heat is lost. It also saves energy."

"No, I didn't know about this network," said Bill, still confused as to where the connection was.

"So if we take this concept into our business lives, as you so well put it Bill, when you said you felt like you were trying to break through ice on your own power," said Diane, "you are like the shark without the rete mirabile. Your level of stress depends on the amount of stress around you; you have no way of regulating it. But once you have a miracle network, that can regulate the excess when it's not needed, then you realize that you can regulate your level of stress at almost any time. Your rete mirabile is in your relationships, your colleagues, your coworkers, and your spouse. Are you still with me?"

"Somewhat," said Bill.

"Just think of Matt," Conrad said, "and how his request for me to talk to you resulted in you meeting these great people here, and now we are all part of your rete mirabile, and you are part of ours. You are not just here to listen to us, it will quickly get to the point where your input will help us all just as much as ours has helped you when you needed it most."

"Exactly, and how your relationship with your best friend Pete acted like such a miracle network system for you for years," said Diane, "and how deeply you felt it when it was gone. I know very well what that loss feels like."

"But you said there was a secret ingredient. So what is it?" Bill said, holding his pen in the air to write it down.

"What makes it all happen is intentionality," said Conrad.

There were deep nods of consent from all around the table. Bill wrote down this point and underlined it.

"In the four tips the marriage counselor gave us," Diane said, "he always added at the end to be 'intentional' about them. We have to be intentional about all of our relationships.

They don't just happen."

Right then a message from Claire popped up on his screen.

Pizza and board games tonight?

This was good. It was a code from Claire to signal that she was 'in', that it was business as usual in their family. It was a tradition they had when the kids were little, and they had continued for a while until a few years ago. In the pauses during the games, as they all took turns, there was an easy chance to exchange and communicate about what had happened that day, or make plans for the next. He didn't know why they had stopped, it was such silly fun. They would play anything from Pictionary to pick up sticks and they would invariably end up rolling with laughter on the family room carpet. What had changed? Yes, the kids had grown up, and the girls had left, but Matt used to love it and so did Claire. Claire intuitively knew about this 'intentionality' Bill thought. She knew how to keep their miracle network going.

Bill said his goodbyes to the group and went out on the dock. There looking out on the deep blue sea, the sun bright overhead, he quickly answered Claire's message the way he always used to... "You're on!"

Yes, they were 'on'. He now had a new clarity. He had been selfish, busy and needy, asking to be served rather than to serve, thinking that the problems of business qualified him to be worthy of extra attention at home, thinking that his work challenges exempted him from being present and available to his family.

He would talk to Claire to see if she'd like to go away on a couples' retreat to invest in their marriage and to hopefully improve or re-establish their communication skills. Claire had been under a great deal of strain lately, trying to read the mixed signs of what Bill had failed to communicate. It was his intention to look after all his relationships, both personal and professional, at home and at work, his own rete mirabile.

Then he remembered what Diane's pastor had said, and he repeated a simple, "Thank you, Jesus!"

CHAPTER 8

Discipline to Spend Quiet Time
Each Morning with God

The girls had already gone back to their respective schools and the family was back down to a unit of three. Matt had gotten up early and already left to help his best friend on moving day. Matt was super excited that his friend's new home was within easy biking distance, so they would not have to rely on their parents 'shuttle service' to spend time with each other, or rather, in front of each other's videogame screens. When Bill came downstairs for breakfast, Claire had already finished hers. He poured himself a cup of coffee, and heard a ruffling sound in the hallway. He found Claire pushing the cardboard box and "group" pictures where they had packed all the photos to clear the room for the plumber to access the wall. Claire had set out the new wallpaper, and the tools. It was a task they had done together before, first in their tiny little rental as newlyweds, then in their one-bedroom apartment as Bill started White Tiger, and once again when they moved here, as the family and the business grew, to their forever home in Claire's dream neighborhood. They had renovated and decorated the home a little at a time, as means allowed, and it had turned out beautifully.

"Can I give you a hand?" Bill said, kissing Claire's shoulder lightly, in a gesture that was so familiar and yet had seemed such a long distance away just a couple of days ago.

"You can give me two," Claire said, handing him the first roll.

Without a word, they both engaged in the dance of helping each other stretch out the paper, hold the ladder, apply the adhesive, and brush out the bubbles. It seemed much easier than the last time Bill had done it. Modern materials, probably.

"Love the color," Bill said. It was a subtle grey stripe over a cream background. He was trying to find a way to broach the subject of marriage counseling, without it sounding like there was a problem between them. It was Claire that gave him the in that he was looking for.

"Yeah, I wanted to ask you before choosing it, but I was miffed at you that day so I picked it out myself. How was your 'Upstairs' lunch?" she said, busy positioning a long strip of paper.

Bill told her about the disciplines and how the group had jelled into a sort of a 'stress less accountability team', and how he now was convinced every CEO should have one.

"It's easy to get stuck in the comfort zone," Claire said, "it takes resolve and discipline to move out of our comfort zone to achieve what we really want. We've always told our kids to stretch their wings, even if it felt uncomfortable or scary at first. I'm really proud that you stuck with the Upstairs group, I know it must have been difficult to open up when things were not going your way."

Bill's eyes became just a little bit shiny, but he didn't look down and kept balancing on the ladder to align the last strip of paper perfectly straight.

"We need a network, a system to help us do what we want to do, and get us back on track if we slip" Bill said, "like when I would say I wanted to be healthy, but then would not exercise or eat properly, or get enough sleep."

"Well, it's hard to get out of a rut, but you did it. Remember when you were just starting and you were great at operations and managing people, but you felt that you would never be able to sell. And then... look at you! You just went out and did it, and got better and better. It's the same with this now, just keep working at acquiring good habits, and you'll get better and better... plus you're getting some exercise now!" said Claire, standing back to admire the finished work.

It looked really good, almost professional. She cleared away the cuttings and pushed forward the box with the photo frames.

"So now, the photo's back up on the wall. Do you remember the position they were in?" said Claire.

"Let's spread them out on the floor exactly how you want them, and then I'll measure and drill the holes." Bill offered a solution to counter his bad memory.

They both sat down on the floor, and started pulling out their precious memories one by one. An hour passed, among giggles and 'Oh-remember-that-one!" laughing at old haircuts and questionable fashion choices. There before them lay a story they had written together, captured in "group" pictures, punctuated by happy moments, obstacles overcome, hard work accomplished, and love. The shared laughter brought their wonderful life to the surface, warming brighter with every memory.

"OK," Bill took one last look at the wall with no pictures but covered with the new wallpaper, "let's do this."

"I'll start lunch while you put up the photos and I'll help you clean up after." Claire let go of Bill's hand in slow motion as she headed toward the kitchen.
Bill hummed to himself to the background muffled sound of Claire moving around in the kitchen. He called her in to see the end result.

"Looks great!" she said, "I'm so happy the house is back to normal."

"So am I, I really, really am," said Bill, and they both understood the deeper meaning of those words.

Just then Matt came into the room and found them locked in each other's arms.

"Hey Matt," Claire said, "How did the moving go?"

"OK, we have a little more stuff in the afternoon. Is it OK if Ethan comes over for lunch?"

"Sure," she said, "we are having pork chops and mashed potatoes. Ready in thirty."

"Awesome! I'll go tell him..." and Matt was off as quickly as he had arrived, but before he left he called out from the kitchen door "the photo-wall looks great!"

"Our kid thinks we are awesome," Claire said.

"I think we're doing pretty well ourselves," Bill laughed. "Let's sit out in the garden until lunch is ready, I have something I wanted to share with you."

--

This time Bill felt different on his way to the Upstairs meeting. Mainly because he had Claire on the passenger seat. The minute Bill had shared the marriage counselor's advice with her and invited her to go on a marriage retreat, she had asked if she might come with him to the next meeting. He had texted Syd to let him know there would be one more guest for lunch, and he sounded so excited to meet Claire that Bill wondered why he hadn't introduced her to the group sooner.

After they said hello and found their seats, conversation quickly turned to the next discipline. It was Conrad himself who had asked that they meet that day, and he had an urgent need for support. It took Bill by surprise, because Conrad was the one who seemed to have all the answers, but on this day he saw him in a new, imperfect but gentler light.

"I am blessed to have such a wonderful support system in all of you," said Conrad. "I really can't give enough credit to you for leading me to the

Discipline to Spend Quiet Time Each Morning with God

disciplines and for the patience to get me back on track when I relapse. See, Bill, we have this discipline to pray and spend quiet time each morning with the Lord. I am finding that the slightest interruption is an excuse to skip that a bit and get on with the urgent matters of the day ahead."

"That's great for Bill, as well, since we haven't yet talked about it, and it's always a tricky one," said Syd.

"What exactly is your definition of quiet time?" Bill asked in a tone that implied he knew but wanted to see if the others had a better answer.

Syd jumped right in, "Quiet time is the time you spend alone communicating with God. This involves both speaking and listening, or rather praying and reading the Bible.

Frankly, it took me years to develop a good habit in this area. I happen to know for sure when I became disciplined with morning quiet time. It was just before we built this extension to the diner here. I've been a Christian and really committed all my life, but the diner was going through a slow patch, people feeling the pinch with the economic downturn, and counting their pennies. One morning, just there looking out on the dock, I handed over control to God. I threw my hands up in the air and said, 'Okay, if this is the way it must be, I'm fine with it. I'll close down the diner and trust that the Lord has a better use for me.' I said 'God, I am putting the business in your hands.' That was it.

Almost overnight, people started pouring in. I tell you, pretty much overnight. People started to ask to book family occasions or business lunches and I ended up having to expand and build this dining room! It's as if God was telling me that he wanted to show me what was possible with my little diner. So I decided that instead of running the diner for myself, I would simply run it for Him and do what He led me to do. Ever since that day, without fail, I spend meaningful quiet time with the Lord each morning. After all, He's running the show. And the more I let Him, the more I have confidence that God can certainly take care of things in my life better than I can. So it only makes sense that

I spend time with God each morning rather than spin my wheels each day trying to 'do' life and business on my own."

"I'm exactly the same," Diane said, "I still have days when I miss my quiet time usually because I have an early meeting or if I'm traveling and away from my normal environment, but when I miss it, oh, how I feel it! Some people say they don't have time to read God's word in the mornings, but I have found that I become more efficient with the rest of my day when I do. For example, when I skip quiet time, my thinking seems to be a little off track and my day seems to get out of whack. I have found that when I invest an hour in the morning in quiet time reading God's word, talking to Him and in reflection, I can get more work done in the following four hours than I can get done in eight hours straight without asking God for favor and guidance."

"I can't help but to work out the math," Claire said, lifting a finger as a professor making a point at a lecture.

"Claire is a teacher," Bill said with a wink.

"With quiet time, you can do in five hours what would have taken eight. That is the same production in only 62.5% of the time. That gives you over one third of your day back for free time, ministry, rest, or to spend time with family," Claire said, and nudged Bill playfully. "As business owners who have goals to achieve, this makes a lot of sense for you."

"I know!" said Conrad, agreeing with Claire, "it really makes sense to all of us, and that's why it is so upsetting to me when I don't follow this discipline, I don't understand what is stopping me. I've put this discipline to the test and always found it to be true. I'm just struggling with it right now."

"That's wh-what we are here for," said Ted, with the slightest stutter.

"Even when we have discipline and good habits forming," said Diane, "challenges surface that can cause these to break down. We can blame it on Satan, since we know he does not want us to accomplish anything that God wants us to do. But, as the Bible says..."

"...th-there is always a way out," said Ted, finishing her sentence.

"So what works for you Ted?" Bill wanted Claire to get a glimpse of Ted's wisdom.

"You'll laugh, but for me it's conversational prayer. I don't stutter when I pray," Ted's speech had become more fluid now, "Instead of making a big deal about praying the 'right way' I just begin talking with God, like I'm talking to you right now. What I have on my plate that day, or a particular stressful situation that I am dreading. I often pray for insight, productivity and efficiency at work."

"I like the sound of that!" said Conrad, "productivity and efficiency. Thank you Ted. Think of how much time I can save when my first decision is the right decision, or when our financials balance the first time through. How about praying for favor with a potential conflict resolution situation?"

"That too," Diane said, "anything really, be it a customer dispute, or filling an open job with the right person. These are the things that you are really thinking about, and these things may come together for us better with some wisdom and discernment received during communication with God."

"I like Proverbs," as everyone's glance shifted to where the voice came from and Syd was sitting. "I read one chapter in Proverbs each day. I simply read the Proverbs that matches the day. For example, I read Proverbs 1 on the first day of the month. Since there are 31 Proverbs, it works well." The room nodded.

"Lately my morning quiet time seems to be nothing but disruptions," said Conrad, "it could be our new puppy,

Cha Cha, wanting attention or chewing through my shoes, or an urgent text message, or a hundred little things. It's gotten to the point where when I settle in for my quiet time, I can feel my body tensing up expecting the interruption to come."

"I once heard a speaker at a sports conference," said Coach Kenner, "share a story about competing in a particularly challenging ironman triathlon. When he was asked what lessons he learned as he fought an unexpected rain storm, a flat tire on his bike and more than normal cramping in his legs and arms, he responded that his experience had taught him to remind himself 'This too shall pass'. This is a good lesson to remember when you are going through a rough patch. This too shall pass. What you can add to it is to pray for understanding. How can you learn from this? What is God's perspective? How is God working? Seeing purpose in difficult times can reduce stress greatly."

"I know this too shall pass. I need to be more intentional about my quiet time." Conrad said, visibly engaged now in the collective wisdom of the group, "While human greed, corruption, and desire for power has created a lot of externally stressful situations at work for many people, my problem seems to be distractions, busyness and wrong focus. A focus away from self to meditating on God's word and how it applies to me is what I need to do. I just need to put my focus back on God and take it off myself. When we get caught up in ourselves too much, we tend to start stressing. That's what is happening to me. See Bill how this works? Even when you're an Upstairs veteran like me, you always need to be reminded of the disciplines."

"It makes me feel better about all my rookie questions," said Bill, "it's so easy to get wrapped up in the urgent and all tied up in a knot about work."

"Exactly!" Conrad said, coming back to his usual energized self. Even his cheeks were changing to a healthier color, "Think about it. What do I have to complain about? Work is a good thing not meant to be stressful! We get to work! We get to own a business! Or rather we get to steward a business God owns! What a privilege!"

There was a hushed pause, as everyone seemed to reflect on that truth. That statement had sent Bill deep into his thoughts. It had struck a chord in a big way. Thinking of White Tiger as really being owned by God and just a tool to do his work, made stress management suddenly seem easier. From now on he could focus on serving, learning and getting better and trust God with the results. If any stressing needs to be done, let God do it. After all, he can handle it better than Bill ever could.

"Takes practice," Coach Kenner said, as if thinking out loud.

"What does?" asked Bill

"Discipline. It takes practice," said the Coach. "To apply each discipline correctly, you need to know yourself – your strengths and weaknesses. I remember going to watch Larry Bird play for the Boston Celtics in his rookie year. He was amazing -who can forget the way he would dribble down to the corner and be forced to do a fade away jump shot, giving us the thrill of watching the basketball go through the hoop and hit nothing but net, all the while, the fans sitting in the front row floor seats, are trying to catch Bird as he falls backwards. I heard the story that one fan later said to Bird that he had the luckiest corner shot in all of basketball. Bird's reply was short and sweet: 'The more I practice, the luckier I get'. He had discipline. Discipline is saying no now, so that you can have something better later. It takes discipline to give up sleeping in for that extra hour of practice. Larry Bird wanted to hit those shots more than he wanted to stay in bed. And in the same way, we have to want our quiet time more than staying in bed a little longer."

Dessert and coffee had already made the rounds and their meeting was now coming to an end as naturally as it had started. Claire took the opportunity to thank everyone for the warm welcome.

"Earlier Conrad said what a blessing you all were to him," Claire said, "and I would just like to say how much I appreciate your support and advice to Bill, that by extension enriches me and my family. I thank you from the bottom of my heart and please know that you are all welcome to our house to celebrate Bill's birthday a week from Saturday."

It was a surprise to Bill that there was a celebration of his birthday in the planning. He was rather avoiding the 'big-five-o' conversation at all costs. He wasn't sure how he felt mixing his business peers with his family and friends... who knows who was on the guest list? He seemed to be the last one to be informed. He should have been flattered, he thought, but he would have preferred a quiet dinner out, or another board-games night.

Anyway, he couldn't unring the bell, Claire had issued the invitation and so there is to be a party, and he would have to be the perfect host as she had a right to expect him to be.

Bill excused himself and dropped Claire at church where she was meeting her Bible study group. He didn't mention the party again, but he couldn't stop thinking about it as he drove away.

CHAPTER 9

Discipline to Get and Keep
Your Financial House in Order

Knowing his first meeting would be with the three brothers, Bill intentionally invested some time praying to begin his day that all would go well and God would grant him favor with his customer. Also, for the first time in years, Bill read in his Bible, beginning with Proverbs chapter one which happens to talk about getting wisdom and understanding; very timely, he thought.

On his way to his meeting with the three brothers, Bill felt slightly apprehensive, but confident, or at least hopeful. There shouldn't be any surprises, Eamon had emailed them the information and had walked them through it on the phone, and they all agreed that the matter had been satisfactorily identified and resolved. Yet they insisted that Bill come over to see them.

Bill hoped that this whole problem would just go away and that the three brothers would be reasonable in their demands. He felt as if he was on the upswing getting a handle on the stress less life, and didn't want anything to get in the way of his 'stress less rehab'.

The meetings with the Upstairs group had helped him identify ways to recognize and manage stress. Identifying the root causes and choosing his response was half the battle. He was sleeping much better and as a result he was raring to go in the morning. He was eating balanced meals, which resulted in snacking less, which in turn meant that his pants were not so tight. The white of his eyes were whiter. He felt lighter, had more energy, and consequently it was easier to move around more. *Funny how these things are linked, we fall into these bad habits and one leads us into another.*

The receptionist ushered Bill to a small meeting room where the three brothers were waiting for him. It looked like the room was used as an informal break room. The three brothers offered Bill a choice of flavors from an espresso machine, and there was a selection of small muffins and diced pineapple on a small platter on a low round table surrounded by soft low armchairs. Bill was quick to notice everything was impeccably clean, gleaming in fact. He felt proud of the good job that his cleaners had obviously done.

"I'll go for the hazelnut, no sugar, thank you," said Bill, sitting on the edge of one of the comfortable chairs.

"We'll cut to the chase, Bill," the more outspoken of the brothers said, bringing him his coffee, "there's a reason why we asked you to come here."

"Yes, I thought there must be, Eamon said he went over the accounts and everything seems to be in order now," Bill said.

"Yes, that's all good and done," said the older brother, "but there's two things we couldn't discuss over the phone and are best said in person."

Here we go, thought Bill, trying his best poker face.

"Maybe three," said the third brother.

"Three things," Bill said, swallowing hard his first sip of coffee.

The first brother leaned forward in his chair.

"First of all we want to apologize," he said, "looking back to our initial conversation; we were way out of line, putting the integrity of your business in question."

He went on to explain how the culprit in the case of the missing medication had been resolved, and it had been a member of their own staff who had been at fault improperly storing and handling their inventory. It had been a coincidence in the timing of the cleaners coming in the previous evening, and the medications found missing by a random spot-check the following morning.

"Furthermore, we want to say thank you," he continued, "for the great job your company is doing day in and day out, and the dignified way in which you handled our complaint. We overreacted and you and Eamon kept a level head throughout. We appreciate it."

Bill nodded, and raised his hand as if to brush away any inconvenience.

"Finally we want to congratulate you," they said, "about your daughter."

So they had made the connection between Amy's application and her father.

"She's a bright young lady and she'll definitely be doing her internship here if she's still interested, she was the most qualified candidate by a long mile. But we just wanted to share with you one thing she said in her interview," the third brother said, "When asked about who her role model or hero was, she said it was you."

There was a silence while Bill absorbed their words. He felt a welling in his chest, working its way up his throat to his eyes.

"You could knock me down with a feather," Bill said, his eyes shining.

"Amy said that what she most admires in you is that you say what you mean and mean what you say, and that your word is as good as gold, and that it is the way she intends to live her life, by those standards."

"Well," Bill said, "Isn't that something... I don't know what to say, it's the best thing any father can hear."

"We thought she might not mention it to you, and so we wanted to make sure you knew. And that you can count on us to tell everyone we know about your business."

Bill couldn't help but think of how this was a huge answer to his morning prayer for favor. The meeting continued for a while, in the same spirit, Bill realizing more and more what a transformation had taken place in his life in a relative short period of time. On his way back to the office to tell Eamon about the meeting, Bill had a flashback to that low moment in the cemetery, where he had felt his health giving way, isolated from everything and everyone that really mattered to him. The events that led to this day seemed ordinary enough, yet had a monumental effect on Bill: his young son Matt mentioning his concern to Conrad in earnest, Conrad taking it seriously enough to invite Bill to meet the group, and the disciplines that Bill firmly believed had turned around his existence from an unceasing cycle of stress and unease to a life that he could look forward to with joy in his heart. These guiding lights that he had now in his life had even saved his relationship with Claire from deteriorating for no particular reason. It was astounding to Bill how miscommunication can drive a wedge between people that are so close, and he was thankful that the disciplines had helped him bridge the distance between them and find their way back to the easy closeness they had always shared. On impulse, he pulled over to call Conrad and say to him how he appreciated the disciplines and the group. When Conrad answered, however, there was something in his voice that urged Bill to ask if everything was all right.

"Everything's fine," Conrad said, "just a little tied up at the moment, I won't be able to make it to lunch."

"Anything I can do to help?" Bill said.

"No, I got it under control," Conrad said, "just the usual ups and downs of a business."

"It sounds more like a 'downs' than an 'ups'," Bill said, "do you mind if I come over?"

Bill called Eamon and told him about the surprising turn of events at the meeting with the three brothers, and that he would be taking a detour to see a fellow business owner. He didn't know why his instinct was telling him to make a point of talking to Conrad in person, except that he kept thinking back to the last meeting, Conrad having trouble with his discipline... it made him wonder if there was something that was troubling Conrad, something he was trying to minimize.

Conrad looked drawn, as if his energy had been somehow sapped. At first he made small talk, asked Bill about the family, the business, and how things were going with the disciplines. That gave Bill the opportunity to ask him about the real cause of his apparent distress.

"It is under control, really," Conrad said, "but I had to set aside a couple of days to tackle some irregularities. Not my favorite thing."

"After our last Upstairs meeting it occurred to me that you actually were under stress," Bill said, "and seeing as that's the whole point of the disciplines, and that I am now a part of your miracle network, here I am."

"You're right," Conrad said, "I was under stress, I still am in a way, but I am coming out of it, and it is thanks to the disciplines. Let me show you the last one, the only discipline that we haven't yet talked about with you, it's probably the next one that will come up anyway."

"What is it about?" Bill was always excited to add one more discipline to his toolbox.

"Finances," Conrad said, "if you Google the word, you'll find it is the top cause of stress in America."

"Doesn't surprise me," said Bill.

"It is also one of the top reasons for the breakdown of relationships and one of the top most quoted causes of divorce and quite frankly business failure."

Bill nodded. Yes, he could understand that too. He had been lucky to have such a supportive wife in Claire, especially when they were struggling to get White Tiger off the ground.

"So as you can imagine this comes up often as one of the most important disciplines, we call it the discipline to get and keep your financial house in order. Come to think of it, this is the only discipline where we produced kind of a cheat-sheet, in writing. I have it on my computer and also on my message board right here."

Discipline to Get and Keep Your Financial House in Order

Conrad reached for a page held up by magnets.

"So are you having trouble with your cash flow?" Bill said.

"I let it get out of hand a little bit," Conrad grunted, "nothing major, but we had a check bounce and that was a red flag. Luckily my relationship with the bank is such that the manager picked up the phone to call me directly."

"It happens," Bill thought about similar incidents in his own business.

Still embarrassing though," Conrad said, "not the image I want my business to present. So I decided to dig in and find what's going on with the books, except that I put it off for a couple of days that turned into over a month, because I actually don't like doing it, and now it's a bit of a dark cloud hanging over me. So I'm sticking to the discipline and I'm not leaving this office until I sort it out. The big thing here is that when the finances are very organized and accurate, it builds confidence - which is good. Many business owners get so busy pleasing customers, running their business, communicating with employees, etc.... that they just keep putting off keeping the books. At some point, this goes on for so long, that they don't even know where to begin to pull it back in shape. While the weight and burden of keeping updated books is tremendous, there always seem to be other things that are more urgent. The urgent takes over, stress rises and the books fall by the wayside.

"I know exactly what you mean," said Bill, "when we had our fracas with the software I felt as if I would rather wrestle a grizzly bear than to open those 'past due' envelopes."

"In our discussion about this discipline with the Upstairs group we all experienced the same thing. The first critical area of business to slide when the leader is suffering from stress seems to be financial management. This triggers a self-perpetuating stressful environment. When a leader gets back to functioning at a high level of motivation they typically enjoy tracking their business progress, comparing the actual results to goals and basically flourish in an environment of keeping score. On the flipside, leaders experiencing stress can become demotivated, evidenced by a lack of interest in knowing how current activity measures up to goal. Financial management is one area of business that requires great discipline and focus to stay current. The problem becomes self - multiplying as business owners get further behind on keeping their books, posting expenses, etc. They become less confident in their sustainability and less effective in how they manage their finances, which produces even more stress. Next thing you know, bills are not getting paid either due to a lack of cash or a lack of organization. The stress meter rises. Taxes need filing and you don't know where to start. The deadline is looming and stress is growing. Business is no longer fun. It's a burden."

It sounded to Bill as if Conrad was reciting these business woes for his own benefit.

"What's worst of all," Conrad said, "is that I know all of this and my entrepreneur personality still allowed me to slip."

"I know, we start feeling sorry for ourselves as if it was an external curse that drove us down that rabbit hole...

if we could just click our heels and be safe again," Bill said, only half-joking. He'd been there, done that.

Bill read the sheet that Conrad had handed over:

Steps to Getting your Financial House in Order

1. Use a qualified CPA/accountant to help you get your books up to date. All income and expenses posted, balance sheet reviewed and correct, bank accounts reconciled, tax returns done. All of this being complete is very freeing and reduces stress.

2. Review financials with a coach to brainstorm how to improve or conclude that all is well.

3. If you don't already have one, outline a plan to achieve and maintain profitable and positive cash flow status.

4. If debt exists, create and follow a plan to eliminate debt. Debt obligations can be stressful for business, especially when the economy dips.

5. Once debt is eliminated, create and follow a plan to build a reserve or emergency fund.

6. Once an emergency fund is established, begin to fund business and personal lifestyle improvements from excess cash flow.

7. With no debt, a healthy reserve fund, positive cash flow and improving personal and business life, stress is significantly reduced.

Bill thought it was really useful information, and that he might rewrite it later, to post it in his office along with his notes about the other disciplines.

"In our years together with the Upstairs group," said Conrad, "we discovered that the best place to start when trying to help a business owner become unstuck from a stressful spiral is to require them to get their financial house in order. Notice, I did not say to get their business profitable. I said, in order."

"I get it," said Bill, "I remember that when we broke even for the first time with White Tiger, I was convinced that we were making a profit, but I had no way of proving it. I had been so busy growing the business, satisfying customers and hiring the right team of cleaners that the books took a back seat. When it came to tax filing time, my poor accountant was tearing his hair out. I was really stressing about it. I had this giant bin stuffed with paperwork and receipts. I had to sit on it to get it to shut. I kept telling myself that I would sort it out over the weekend, except I was exhausted and our small children needed my attention. One day I didn't have the money in the bank to meet payroll that week. That shook me out of my stubbornness to not ask for help."

"What happened?" Conrad asked.

"The simplest solution, I hired Eamon. When he saw the plastic bin for the first time, he actually rolled on the floor laughing."

"A sense of humor at the right time in the right place can be a great stress relief," said Conrad.

"He was a Godsend, literally, I bumped into him at a church function. Making small talk after the service he happened to mention that he was a bookkeeper. I asked him if he could take one more client and he said he'd come to see me the following day. I'm not making it up. I was all serious and embarrassed, and he was new and trying to make a good impression. When he asked me to show him the system I was using, I pointed to the bin and he reached down and opened it. It was then that I saw his shoulders started shaking, his knees buckled and he held his belly as he laughed, and laughed, and laughed, until we were both laughing together kneeling next to the mounds of paper. I knew I had the right man for the job. It took him ten full working days to sort out the mess and balance the books. He started coming one day a week, and over the years he's now full time and has been my right hand ever since."

"Make sure to let him know how much you appreciate his work," said Conrad.

"I do," said Bill, "so how about if we go to lunch, and then I come back here and help you get started," Bill said. "You know, get your bin under control, in a manner of speaking."

"Well I don't know..." Conrad said, "I guess... You know what? I'm starving!"

By now Conrad had regained the spring in his step and when they were seated at the table Bill noticed that he was back to his affable, open and communicative self.

Naturally the discipline discussed that lunchtime was keeping the financial house in order. Syd was particularly focused on never letting his finances slip.

"Keeping accurate and current financial reports, including daily or at minimal weekly posting of income and expenses, as well as at least monthly review of income statements and balance sheets, increases the chances of business health and sustainability tremendously," Syd said. "So that's the reason we made it into a discipline and we put together that cheat sheet that Conrad showed you. Plus, the confidence of knowing where you stand financially is a stress diluter."

"It is so logical," Bill said, "that you would think it would be the thing every business owner would subscribe to."

"Well, it comes natural to me," said Syd, "but for many people the financials just... let's say it's not their passion or strength, so they let it slide. It's also not as urgent as closing the deal or satisfying the customer. Procrastination with the finances subconsciously takes over and before long, it's just a source of trouble and stress. If you want to subscribe to stressing less, you must have the discipline to put a financial management system in place to keep you in the know and confident of where you stand financially.

This doesn't automatically create or even guarantee an increase in profitability, but at least you will understand why, and likely have the information you need to begin corrective action."

By the end of their meeting, Bill had one more question for the group.

"You know how I've been keeping notes and posting them in my office," Bill said, "about the disciplines, so it occurred to me that the only discipline that has something in writing is this one we talked about today, about finances, but all the others are equally important."

Everybody nodded and made enthusiastic approving noises, Bill knew he had hit a nerve.

"I believe strongly that it would be very useful and important to have a 'go-to' reading summarizing everything about the nine disciplines we've discussed here. I would like to volunteer, if you're all in agreement, to prepare a handout summarizing each one."

To Bill's surprise, they all started clapping, saying, yeah! Great idea! Sounds good!

"Tell you what," said Conrad, "that's such a great idea that we'll make it the tenth discipline. To keep a go-to reading list about the disciplines, and we shouldn't stop there, it could extend beyond the disciplines to any useful reading that supports a stress less business."

Just like that, Bill felt as if he had been promoted from junior apprentice to full member of the group. He was in charge of coming up with his own contribution to the Upstairs group: the newest discipline.

After lunch before joining Conrad to help him with his numbers, Bill swung back by the office. Eamon was waiting.

"Sit yourself down boss," Eamon said, "I have good news."

"This day just keeps getting better," Bill proclaimed.

"With the software back up and being able to track financials again, I've identified two loss centers. In other words, I confirmed that you were right on those two customers that you suspected were not profitable."

Bill literally felt a lifting of a weight off his shoulders. He sat straighter in his chair. He had discussed this a few times with Eamon, but not having the numbers at his fingertips to know if he was right or not, they had dared not make any changes. Eamon suggested a few points to correct the situation without losing the customers. Bill now had a plan of action. He couldn't help thinking back to the stacks of unposted, unpaid and unfiled financials in that plastic bin. How differently the story of his business could have unfolded.

"Second good news," Eamon said, "a potential new customer called today, referred by the three brothers. Put that in your pipe and smoke it!"

"What a turnaround!" Bill said.

He felt a new sense of purpose and focus. His business was growing, and yet he was stressing less. The Upstairs club couldn't have arrived at a more opportune time. Now he not only felt grateful to receive the disciplines but he felt part of a miracle network with value to bring to others, and he was starting right now, on his way to support Conrad to get his financial house in order. Amazing.

CHAPTER 10

Discipline to Have Preset Go-To Reading for Encouragement and Focus

Calm. This would be the word for this feeling. There was no sound but the chirping of birds and a soft breeze rustling across the poplars. Bill rested his hand on Pete's tombstone, as he did each time he visited, his palm flat on the cool granite. I am well, Pete. You would be so happy for me. *I am well, at peace, working hard but with less stress.*

Tomorrow is my birthday and I'll be missing you buddy. But I won't be sad, because you wouldn't approve of that. You were one of the true shining lights in this world.

Bill had spent the last two evenings writing down the ten disciplines with Claire's help, summarizing what he had heard at the meetings, checking and double-checking that he hadn't left anything out. Now he sat on the bench nearest to Pete's grave, to read over the document one more time. He realized he was sitting in the same spot where he had sat with Conrad in dire distress. What a difference just a few months could make. It was almost difficult for Bill to remember why he had been in such bad shape back then and almost collapsed under the weight of the stress. What was it that had stretched him so thin, to the point of causing him physical pain in his chest? The emotional shock of losing Pete was of course understandable, but the downward spiral of stress in his business and family life felt so far away now that he could almost not believe he was the same person. And yet...

Nothing really earth-shattering had changed. None of the dark clouds that he had feared ever turned into disasters. The crisis at work had been resolved, and there would surely be many more to come, but now he felt much better equipped to face them. He had a fortunate escape with his health. Small adjustments: sleeping a little better, eating a little healthier, exercising a little more, as well as praying and reading God's word. His closeness with Claire was back, this feeling of togetherness, of being passengers travelling side by side on the same journey. There was no high drama in his life, nothing a passerby would think extraordinary. He was on his way to work, stopping to visit the grave of a dear friend. Later he would go to lunch with a group of business peers. On Saturday he would be celebrating his 50th birthday at home, grilling hamburgers in his backyard with his family and guests.

Bill read again the inscription on Pete's headstone, Proverbs 3:5-6, and immediately looked it up on his phone Bible app. "*Trust in the Lord with all your heart and lean not on your own understanding. In all your ways acknowledge him and he will make your paths straight.*" Bill slowly shook his head as he realized how far off path he had been and how the upstairs group had helped him shift from trusting in his own understanding to trusting God. He felt he was finally on the straight path.

"Thanks, buddy," Bill said aloud and then walked away.

At lunch, Bill was eager to share with everyone the document he had prepared. It looked so simple, just words typed out and printed on white copy paper. Yet they had saved his life. If these disciplines had done this for him, he was convinced they could help other people too. This document was his testimony, his contribution to the group that had given him such a treasure of wisdom.

"Okay, let's have it," said Conrad when everyone was seated around the table. "What have you got for us?"

"First let me say what an honor it is for me to be adding my grain of sand to the group's work," said Bill, handing out the photocopies. "The disciplines you've shared with me have helped me so much that I can't even remember the reason why I used to stress so much before. It got me thinking, that when we are stressed and in a funk, it becomes harder and harder to make good decisions. It's as if everything gets out of focus. So by having these disciplines typed up with notes on each one, and why they are important, and how to tap into them when we've gone off track means that we can pull them out in times of need. Just knowing they are there would help us calm down and refocus on what we already know to be effective. We know they work, we just need to remember how.

> **Discipline to Have Go-To Reading for Encouragement and Focus**

We don't want to be deciding what is important to us when we are stressed out. We may also add our 'go-to' scripture reading for encouragement. So that way we have a 'trail of breadcrumbs' that brings us back to the center, where we can regroup and make decisions from a stress less mindset."

"Makes a lot of sense," Diane said, "I always keep updating a go-to list of scripture readings for encouragement. If I try to find readings when I really need them, the paradox is that I am not in the right frame of mind, I am ruffled, distracted by whatever is troubling me. With this go-to reading list all I have to do is remember to pick it up and trust that there was a reason why I chose those scriptures. It works, every time. Good job, Bill, bringing us the discipline to keep coming back to the disciplines."

"Exactly," said Bill, laughing, "this is a discipline about being disciplined to use the disciplines. I love the idea of your go-to scriptures. I think the two would go well together, for each of us to find what speaks to us, what brings us back to center. So here it is. I labeled it The Upstairs Manifesto, to properly honor our special group.

I made a copy for each of us and of course I encourage you to share this with others.

Conrad with a big grin lifts his glass of iced tea signaling a toast, and as others caught on and lifted their lunch drinks, he looked at the group and Bill,

The Upstairs Manifesto
Ten Guiding Disciplines for a Stress Less Business & Life

1: Replace Bad Emotions with Good Emotions

We should focus on controlling our internal response to an external situation. If we do not want our emotions to be stressed, we must give them a replacement feeling, such as patience or love.

2: Work Ahead and Don't Procrastinate

Procrastinating high priority items is not good, creates stress and ultimately reduces quality. It is a luxury that most business owners can't afford. Working ahead produces confidence, increases quality and helps bring joy back to business.

3: Identify and Eliminate Stress Triggers

What needs to change for it not to be this way? Eliminating much of the business-related stress in your life could sometimes be only a few organizational or operational steps away.

4: Get a Good Night's Sleep

Proverbs 3:21-24 provides a Bibilical formula for a good night's sleep. Pray for wisdom, understanding, sound judgement and discretion. As a bonus, pray this for your spouse, children, employees and others who are important in your life.

5: Celebrate Progress, not Perfection

Reducing or eliminating stress in your life is as simple as making sure that you are measuring or viewing life correctly. Much of our stress in life is self-inflicted.

6: Learn from Mistakes and Not Dwell on Them

Dwelling on mistakes or the past creates feelings of regret, frustration or even anger, which are stress triggers. We must gain from mistakes by learning from them and moving on.

7: Invest in Quality and Loving Relationships

Good, quality and peaceful relationships are critical to living with less stress, especially with your spouse, if married. We must be intentional in this area.

8: Spend Quiet Time Each Morning with God

Investing time each morning talking with God and giving your day to Him can actually help you be more productive, efficient and fruitful.

9: Get and Keep your Financial House in Order

When finances are very organized and accurate, it builds confidence. When finances slide, this triggers a self-perpetuating stressful environment.

10: Have Go-to Preset Reading for Encouragement and Focus

We pull this out for encouragement and to help us calm down and refocus. We don't want to be deciding what is important to us when we are stressed out.

"Cheers to Bill for capturing so well what has blessed all of us and especially to God almighty. No matter what comes our way, He always provides."

In unison, everyone responded, "Cheers." Bill sipped from his glass of water and thought of how blessed he truly was.

As Saturday dawned, Bill got busy preparing the backyard party. Claire had rented a tent with tables and chairs. Matt and his best friend had been recruited for grill assistant duty, as well as to prep and pass around the burgers, so Bill could focus on the cooking. They were expecting about forty people, and that was a lot of hamburgers! But you could trust Claire to think of everything, and the rental equipment had arrived and was being set up. Amy and Mary Anne arrived their hands full with party decorations and a huge sheet-cake. There was something else in the car, someone actually. Mary Anne ran up to Bill and hugged him.

"Happy Birthday Dad!"

"Thank you honey!" Bill said, looking over Mary Anne's shoulder at the approaching young man with the tiniest smile on his face.

"Dad, this is Phillip," she said, and Bill could see Matt making faces behind the two, and Amy giving Phillip a thumbs up from a distance. Bill got the picture. Things were serious.

"Welcome, Phillip!" Bill said, trying to brush away a mental flash-forward of Mary Anne married with toddlers calling him Grandpa... "I'm so glad you could make it, it's great to have another hand at the grill! Let me show you the rig..."

When they were out of earshot of the girls, Phillip cleared his throat.

"Bill, sorry to parachute on your party without warning," he said, "Mary Anne wanted it to be a surprise. So it wouldn't be too formal."

"I agree, it made the day even more perfect. We knew that Mary Anne had met someone special, we were looking forward to meeting you. Tell me about yourself."

"I'll give you the elevator speech," Phillip said, "I run a business, a tech startup I launched with a partner just after I got my MBA. We develop the interface for medical applications. We're a small team but it's growing like crazy, so I keep pretty busy."

"I have no idea what that is but it sounds promising," Bill said.

"Actually, Mary Anne mentioned that you are an entrepreneur," Phillip said, "and that you're really great at keeping your business stress free."

Bill felt a sudden wave of pride swelling in his heart. Yes, he was now really good at the stress less business disciplines. The fact that his children had noticed meant that the disciplines had made a difference for his family too. Bill had hoped that this was the case, but here was confirmation.

"Do you feel as if stress is an issue for you in your business?" Bill looked at Phillip. Phillip nodded. Bill recognized the gesture of a concerned business owner. No words, head up and down. That meant a definite yes.

"Then I have some information that you may find useful," Bill said, "it's very simple, ten disciplines that you can incorporate into your work and personal life. They made a big difference to me. Just a few months ago you would have met a very different Bill."

"Really? That would be so great," Phillip said, "I'm okay so far but the business is growing much faster than we thought. We are the victims of our own success. We may even go public. Technology moves quickly. We need to ride the wave, but not let it drown us. I'm starting to wake up in the middle of the night stressed out..."

"I know exactly what you mean," Bill said, thinking back to the nights that would find him wide awake at three in the morning, running through mental lists of issues and possible solutions.

"Anyway," said Phillip. "Enough about me, there'll be plenty of time to bore you with the details, but priorities now, we have a party to take care of."

Phillip turned out to be a practiced hand at handling big parties, being the eldest of six brothers and sisters, he teamed up seamlessly with the rest of the family unit and in no time the tables were covered in bright red and white checkered tablecloths, with centerpieces of yellow daisies in clay pots, jam jar glasses, and the tent and salad table were trimmed in blue and white striped streamers. The backyard with its neatly mowed lawn, tidy flowerbeds, the sparking pool, and the party set up looked the picture of a happy occasion.

Bill was astonished at how excited he felt about his fiftieth birthday party. While earlier on he had dreaded the idea of making a big deal about it, when the day came he was the happiest man on earth. Yes. His family was making a big fuss about his turning fifty, and that was just fine with him! The party was a roaring success, Eamon was there with his wife, Claire's best friends and their husbands, and the entire Upstairs group showed up, bearing two gifts.

Conrad handed him the first, beautifully wrapped. Bill opened it to discover a framed version of The Upstairs Manifesto for a Stress Less Business. Diane then handed him the second gift, in an elegant navy blue flat box tied with a thick gold-colored silk ribbon.

Bill opened it carefully, removing the layers of pale blue tissue paper.

"I can't believe it!" Bill laughed out loud, "You remembered!"

Inside was a crisp linen shirt with flat pockets, Bill recognized the same shirt that Conrad had been wearing that first day at Pete's funeral, the one he had admired. Except this one had Bill's initials finely embroidered in the same tone on one of the pockets.

"Your very own personalized Guayabera!" Diane said.

Bill was so touched that they had organized this surprise, but more than anything that they were all here together in a show of support. They knew how far he had come on the wings of the ten disciplines, and he felt that he was now a full-fledged member of the group that could help so many others in turn. He felt as if his heart couldn't get any fuller.

Later on, as Amy brought out the cake, Bill looked around in wonder. His friends and family all were relaxed, smiling, having enjoyed delicious food, plenty of laughter, and uplifting conversation. How could he have ever been too stressed to notice the absolute wealth of love and spirit that surrounded him? Amy set down the cake with a flourish amid a round of applause, and Bill was amazed at the decoration. The entire top surface of the cake was a sugar printed version of the photo of the family ski trip that was on the picture wall in the hall. The photo they all loved so much, where Bill was at the center of his family and they all looked hopeful, and cheerful. On the bottom was the caption in icing sugar: "He just keeps getting better!"

Bill looked up across the cake at Claire, both had shiny eyes, hers were back to their usual beautiful pool of warm blue.

"Thanks to all of you for coming today," Bill called out to his guests, "and to my wonderful family for putting this together... I feel so blessed. Also," as he looked up to the clouds, "a big thank you to God almighty for saving my life... and to your upstairs angels here on earth, a group of very disciplined angels... you know who you are. Thank you."

The members of the Upstairs group let out a collective chuckle.

Bill then skipped a step closer to his wife, and took her hand, and brought her close by his side. Claire rested her head on his shoulder, just like she had in the old photo.

"To my beautiful, fantastic Claire... what can I say? You know this is my favorite photo of our family, because we look so well, and happy. But you know what? Looking at you all right now and at wonderful family and friends, we are just beginning the rest of our stress less life and many new pictures." Bill and Claire smiled at each other then began waving their hands to signal all their guests to come closer and shouted, "Group picture, everyone!"

Acknowledgements

Sylvia Edwards Davis, my creative writer, for your brilliant imagination.

Amy Boll, Leslie Ogle, Sherry Prewitt and Jeff Burridge, for all your help with this project, the design, good ideas and layout.

Brian Paul, Dick Ollek, Julie Hirschauer, Troy Hopkins, Lyle Graddon, Dan Shock, Fred Paris and Brad Johansson for reading the draft version and providing great feedback.

Michelle and the boys for putting up with all the intense stress I created over the years.

Pastor Q – who inspired and challenged me in January 2016 to pick a word to claim and commit to for the year. I chose "stress less".

Jesus Christ, my Lord and Savior, the ultimate source of true peace, joy and the stress less life.

Commercial Cleaning Services

Office Pride faith-based Franchise
Opportunities are available nationwide.

be a
part
of

**something
great**®

For more information contact us at:
Office Pride Commercial Cleaning Services

(727) 754-5990

Or visit us at:
www.OfficePrideFranchise.com